RODALE'S
SUCCESSFUL ORGANIC GARDENING®
CONTROLLING
WEEDS

RODALE'S
SUCCESSFUL ORGANIC GARDENING®
CONTROLLING WEEDS

ERIN HYNES

Rodale Press, Emmaus, Pennsylvania

Our Mission

We publish books that empower people's lives.

RODALE BOOKS

Copyright © 1995 by Weldon Russell Pty Ltd

If you have any questions or comments concerning this book, please write to:

Rodale Press
Book Readers' Service
33 East Minor Street
Emmaus, PA 18098

Library of Congress Cataloging-in-Publication Data

Hynes, Erin.
    Controlling weeds / Erin Hynes
        p.   cm. — (Rodale's successful organic gardening)
    Includes index.
    "A Kevin Weldon production"—T.p. verso.
    ISBN 0–87596–667–5 hardcover — ISBN 0–87596–668–3
paperback
        1. Weeds—Control. 2. Plants, Protection of. 3. Organic
gardening. I. Title. II. Series.
    SB611.H96 1995
    635'.04958—dc20   95–1597
                                                CIP

Printed in the United States of America on acid-free ∞, recycled paper ♲

Rodale Press Staff:
    Editorial Director, Home and Garden Books: Margaret Lydic Balitas
    Editor: Nancy J. Ondra
    Copy Editor: Carolyn R. Mandarano
    Editor-in-Chief: William Gottlieb

Produced for Rodale Press by Weldon Russell Pty Ltd
107 Union Street, North Sydney NSW 2060, Australia
a member of the Weldon International Group of Companies

    Chief Executive: Elaine Russell
    Publisher: Karen Hammial
    Managing Editor: Ariana Klepac
    Editorial Assistant: Cassandra Sheridan
    Horticultural Consultant: Cheryl Maddocks
    Copy Editor: Yani Silvana
    Designer: Honor Morton
    Typesetter: Rachel Smith
    Picture Researcher: Elizabeth Connolly
    Illustrators: Tony Britt-Lewis, Barbara Rodanska
    Indexer: Michael Wyatt
    Production Manager: Dianne Leddy

A KEVIN WELDON PRODUCTION

Distributed in the book trade by St. Martin's Press

    4 6 8 10 9 7 5 3   hardcover
2 4 6 8 10 9 7 5 3 1   paperback

Opposite: *Rhus typhina* 'Laciniata'
Half title: *Viola labradorica* and *Milium effusum* 'Aureum'
Opposite title page: *Taraxacum officinale*
Title page: *Ipomoea purpurea*
Opposite contents: *Cirsium vulgare*
Contents: *Rhus typhina* (left), *Sonchus oleraceus* (right)
Back cover: *Ipomoea purpurea* (bottom)

CONTENTS

INTRODUCTION

Few things make a landscape look as neglected and unkempt as weeds do. A weedy yard can make an otherwise attractive house look ratty—you know, the kind of place kids are afraid to stop at when they trick-or-treat on Halloween. But the harm weeds do is more than cosmetic; among other things, weeds compete with desirable plants (and usually win), and they shelter pests that can attack garden plants.

It's no wonder that chemical herbicides—weed killers—for home use have found such a warm reception at garden centers. These products promise a weed-free lawn the easy way. But the truth is, weeds aren't that hard to control using methods that are far less harmful to humans and the environment. In most situations, an effective weed control strategy requires more brains than brawn. Once you know what weeds you have and how they grow, it's just a matter of attacking them when they are most vulnerable, then taking steps to keep them from coming back.

As you prepare to battle weeds, set realistic expectations. You'll never get rid of all of your weeds forever. No matter how carefully you weed your own property, new weed seeds arrive continuously, carried by the wind or animals. And you don't necessarily want to eliminate all of the weeds, either. Wild plants—including weeds—contribute to the botanical diversity that helps balance our ecosystems. They also have more obvious benefits, such as providing shelter for wildlife and keeping exposed soil from washing away.

So accept that some weeds are natural and healthy, and decide just how much weediness you can tolerate in the different parts of your yard: the vegetable garden, the lawn, ornamental beds with flowers, trees, and shrubs, and places that don't get much use. If one of those areas has a seemingly hopeless weed infestation that makes you consider moving to a high-rise, *Rodale's Successful Organic Gardening: Controlling Weeds* will guide you to the best method for taming it. And once you get the weeds under control, it gives you ideas for preventing future invasions. After you've explored the wide range of options available for controlling and preventing weeds organically, you'll be able to resist the urge to buy chemical quick fixes, and you'll have a healthier garden, too.

Weed control is a critical part of keeping your garden healthy and looking good. Controlling weeds when they're small or preventing them from sprouting in the first place will make the job much easier.

HOW TO USE THIS BOOK

*R*odale's Successful Organic Gardening: Controlling *Weeds* is your guide to controlling and preventing weeds in every area of your yard. In these pages, you'll read about a variety of methods for getting rid of weeds, and you'll learn how to choose the best method for handling the weeds you have.

This book is divided into two sections. The first half explains what weeds are and how they grow and gives suggestions for dealing with them in the vegetable garden and lawn; around flowers, trees, and shrubs; and in fence lines, paths, and paving.

In "Learning about Weeds," starting on page 12, you'll find out just what you're up against when you take on weeds. You'll learn what makes a plant a weed—the definition is broader than you might think! You'll discover that weeds are harmful in several ways: They compete with desirable plants, shelter insect pests, look unattractive, and more. But weeds aren't *all* bad—they help stop erosion, provide wildlife habitat, and can tell you about your soil's health. Some are even edible! You'll read about the ways weeds are beneficial as well as harmful. And you'll learn some basics of weed identification, which will help you when you take a close look at the weeds growing in your yard.

"Weed Control Options," starting on page 22, explains how to plan a strategy for preventing and controlling weeds around your yard. The first step is to find out how long the plant usually lives because its life cycle is a clue to the best way to get rid of it. This chapter also describes the different methods you can use to prevent and control weeds organically, including mulching, pulling, hoeing, solarizing the soil, using grazing animals, and spraying with organic herbicides. It also includes ideas for maintaining low-maintenance areas, where at least some weeds are welcome.

Vegetable gardens and fruit plantings are two places where weed damage really shows up: If unchecked, a weed infestation can dramatically cut into your harvest. Starting on page 42, "Weeds in the Vegetable Garden" explains how to prevent and control weeds in vegetable gardens, small fruit plantings, and home orchards. It describes the best mulches to use around food crops and explains how a smother crop can get rid of tough weeds. And it shows how to plant and care for your vegetable garden and fruit plantings to discourage weeds from getting a start.

"Weeds in Ornamental Plantings," starting on page 52, tells you the best ways to keep weeds out of flower beds and away from trees and shrubs. It also explains how the flowers and woody plants (trees, shrubs, and vines) you grow can become weedy and what to do about it if they do.

A lush, weed-free lawn is part of the American dream. In "Weeds in Lawns and Groundcovers," starting on page 64, you'll discover that although no lawn is truly free of weeds, you can have a lawn you're proud of without dousing it with chemicals. Keeping your lawn healthy with the proper care explained in this chapter is the most important thing you can do to prevent and get rid of weeds. You'll also learn which control methods are best for coping with individual weeds. For lawns that are too weedy to reclaim, the chapter includes instructions on starting over the right way. And if you've given up some grass in favor of easy-care groundcovers, you'll find tips for preventing and controlling weeds in those plantings.

Weeds have a way of creeping unnoticed into parts of the landscape we take for granted, such as paved areas, walkways, and fence lines. Starting on page 72, "Weeds in Fence Lines, Paths, and Paving" gives tips for preventing and getting rid of ugly weeds in these often-overlooked spots. It also gives suggestions for reclaiming neglected areas such as overgrown meadows and abandoned gardens.

Plant by Plant Guide

The second half of the book is the "Guide to Weeds," which has color photographs and descriptions of more than 140 weeds. With this guide, you'll be able to track down the identity of nearly any garden weed you're likely to encounter. Identifying your weeds is an important step in planning an effective control strategy.

The "Guide to Weeds" is arranged in alphabetical order by botanical name, since the same weed may have many common names. (If you want to look up a weed by its common name, refer to the index.) Each entry includes a color photograph and a description for easy identification, as well as suggestions for controlling the weed. The diagram below shows you what to look for on these informative pages.

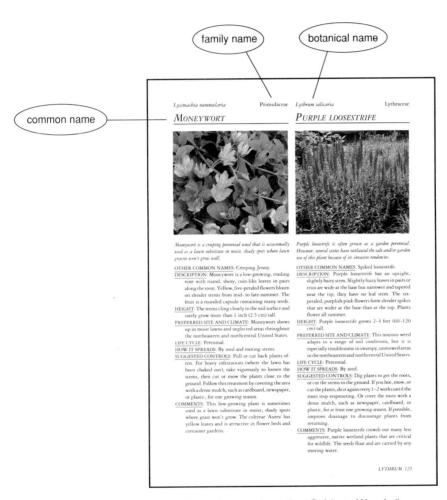

Sample page from the "Guide to Weeds."

LEARNING ABOUT WEEDS

Benjamin Franklin obviously wasn't thinking about gardening when he wrote that nothing is certain in life except death and taxes. In gardening, few things are more certain than weeds.

Weeds can cause gardeners more tearing of hair and gnashing of teeth than any other garden pest. Not only do they look bad but they also compete against the plants we want to grow, stealing the light, water, and nutrients our "good" plants need. Weeds can harbor diseases and insects that attack garden plants and may be poisonous to humans or animals. Some weeds even release chemicals that are toxic to nearby plants.

But despite the long list of problems weeds can cause, they aren't all bad. Weeds grow where many other plants won't, covering soil that would otherwise be bare and could wash or blow away easily. They provide food and shelter for a wide array of good insects that prey on garden pests. Edible weed species can provide food for people. And some, dare we say, are even pretty enough to be grown in low-maintenance areas.

In "What Is a Weed?" on page 14, you'll learn about what makes a particular plant a weed, so you can plan your control strategy accordingly. "The Trouble with Weeds" on page 16 explains in detail why weed control is so important to maintaining a healthy, productive garden. But before you get overwhelmed by the seemingly impossible task of getting rid of all of your weeds, read "In Praise of Weeds" on page 18 to find out how some weeds can actually work *for* you.

If you have a weed problem, you need to know just what you're up against before you can attack it. The first step is to identify the troublesome weeds, and you don't have to be a botanist to do it. "Knowing Your Weeds" on page 20 cuts through the jargon to tell you just what you need to know, so you can figure out what weeds you have to deal with. With a little practice, you'll pick out distinguishing traits quickly and be well on your way to choosing an effective control.

Identifying your problem weeds is the key to choosing an effective control. Common burdock (*Arctium minus*), for instance, is a biennial, so you can dig up the root or cut plants down until they stop resprouting.

What Is a Weed?

Ever since early humans domesticated plants some 4,000 years ago, gardeners have been arguing over which plants are weeds. There are a few plants—like poison ivy—that almost everyone agrees are weeds. But in many cases, the plant in question has some redeeming feature, like pretty flowers or tasty leaves, that clouds the issue. One person complains about having to weed Queen-Anne's-lace out of a vegetable garden; another praises the plant's delicate beauty in a wildflower meadow.

To stop this quibbling once and for all, here is the true definition of a weed: A weed is any plant growing where you don't want it. What plant it is doesn't matter as much as where it is. For instance, if a seed from a tomato you let rot in the garden last year has grown into a tomato plant in this year's zinnia bed, it's a weed. If the bermuda grass you grow as lawn is creeping into your shrub bed, it's a weed. On the other hand, if the dandelion and yarrow and chicory and teasel and mullein and assorted grasses growing in the vacant lot next door strike you as pretty, they are not weeds—at least not until someone goes to build a house on the lot and wants a lawn instead of a wildflower meadow.

Why Weeds Are a Problem

Although virtually every plant has the potential of being a weed in some place or another, some plants are considered weeds more often than others. They may have traits that everyone agrees are undesirable, such as burs that stick to clothing or pollen that makes people sneeze. Some weeds produce toxic compounds that irritate your skin or even cause death if eaten. Others just have a knack for growing where they really look bad—in a flower garden or in paved areas that are a pain to maintain. Some are so vigorous that they crowd out desirable plants.

Can tomato plants be weeds? Yes, if they sprout up in your flower garden.

Field bindweed has attractive flowers, but this tough-to-control, spreading plant is by all accounts a weed.

Trees, shrubs, and vines growing in the wrong place can be some of the most frustrating weeds. Seedlings of trees and shrubs that pop up in the lawn and garden often have tough, woody stems that make them hard to pull up by hand. And vines have a way of twisting around structures and other plants, so removing them becomes as much fun as untangling a mass of fishing line.

How Weeds Succeed

Some plants are considered weeds because they are so widespread. Common weeds are widespread because they are better at surviving than other plants. They may be particularly well adapted for getting water, light, and nutrients or for using those resources in a particularly efficient way. They may be better able to resist diseases and insects or to tolerate a wider range of growing conditions.

Other weeds are widespread because they are simply better at multiplying than most cultivated plants. They may produce more seed or have seed that can travel farther—perhaps in the wind or by being attached to an animal's fur. The seed may be able to live for years in the soil, waiting for just the right conditions to sprout and grow. Some weeds can spread even without producing seed. They may have aboveground runners (called stolons) or underground creeping shoots (called rhizomes), both of which have buds where new plants can start.

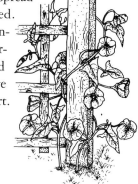

Morning glories (*Ipomoea* spp.) are pretty on trellises, but they can be weeds if they reseed.

Many weeds drop seeds that live for years buried in the soil. When you turn the soil, the weed seeds can sprout.

Wild brambles spread by seed and suckers, so you'll need to control the seedlings as well as the creeping roots.

Where Weeds Appear

Whatever methods weeds use to survive and spread, a quick look around gives evidence as to how successful they are. You can find weeds almost anywhere. Home gardeners battle them in their lawns, flower and shrub beds, and vegetable gardens—even in sidewalks and driveways. Farmers fight them in crop fields and pastures. Roadsides, abandoned fields, fencerows, and waste areas are usually covered with weeds.

Any time you expose bare soil—such as when you till the vegetable garden or prepare a new flower bed—you're providing an open invitation for plant growth. Ideally, you want your garden plants—the vegetables, fruits, flowers, or lawn—to thrive in the site. And if you've chosen plants adapted to that site, prepared the soil well, and planted and mulched them properly, your desirable plants have every chance to do just what you want them to.

The problem arises when that bare soil is more favorable to weeds than to the plants you want to grow. The location may be too sunny or shady, too cool or too hot. The soil may be too acid or alkaline, too low in fertility, or too wet or dry. If animals or people have walked over the same area repeatedly, the soil may be compacted, making it difficult for many plants to get the water and oxygen their roots need. If you haven't chosen plants that can adapt to those conditions or haven't taken steps to correct them, you can be sure that at least one weed will be happy to make a home there.

Annual and biennial weeds reproduce by making lots of seed. Preventing them from flowering is the key to control.

Not all unplanted plants are weeds. These perennials reseeded in the paving, creating a charming, casual look.

The Trouble with Weeds

It only takes a quick glance and a slight appreciation for aesthetics to know that weeds can make a lawn or garden look ratty. But the problems with weeds go further than simply offending our sensibilities.

Unhealthy Competition

Weeds, like any other plants, need a few things to survive: light, water, oxygen, and nutrients. Unfortunately for the gardener, weeds are often better adapted to searching out these things than our desirable plants. Vigorous weeds shoot upward in their search for sunlight, often shading out the leaves of slower-growing garden plants. And because weeds often have aggressive, spreading roots, they can use up the soil's supply of water, nutrients, and oxygen before other plants get to them.

This competition is more damaging at certain times than at others. New garden plants in particular need all of the protection they can get from weeds while they establish healthy root systems. And plants demand more light, water, and nutrients when they flower and set fruit than at other times, so these are also essential periods to keep weeds under control.

Some weeds are especially dirty fighters—they release chemicals that are toxic to other plants. This trick of producing toxic chemicals is called allelopathy; plants that do it—like quack grass (*Agropyron repens*)—are said to be allelopathic. The toxins may be released from the roots or wash into the soil from fallen leaves. The allelopathic chemicals can kill seedlings or stunt growing plants. One clue that a plant might be allelopathic is a bare area beneath it; this is especially obvious near allelopathic trees, such as a black walnut.

Poisonous Plants

Some weeds go beyond producing chemicals that are toxic to other plants: They release substances that are poisonous to humans and animals.

Among the most notorious poisonous plants are those that cause skin rashes, such as poison ivy (*Toxicodendron radicans*), poison sumac (*T. diversilobum* and *T. toxicarium*), and

Yellow toadflax (*Linaria vulgaris*) is attractive, but its spreading roots crowd out most companions.

poison oak (*T. vernix*). Their leaves and stems contain extraordinarily potent oils that cause blisters even with secondhand contact—for example, if you pet an animal that has brushed against the plant.

Some weeds are poisonous if you eat them. There's poison hemlock (*Conium maculatum*), which Socrates was forced to ingest. And there's pokeweed (*Phytolacca americana*), with a root so deadly that one mouthful can

Common pokeweed (*Phytolacca americana*) produces clusters of poisonous berries; the roots are toxic, too.

kill you. Some poison indirectly: Cows that eat white snakeroot (*Eupatorium rugosum*) give milk that causes milk sickness, which killed Abraham Lincoln's mother.

The pollens that cause hay fever aren't poisons, but they sure can make people miserable. In much of the United States, the pollen of ragweed (*Ambrosia* spp.) is the biggest troublemaker. Bermuda grass (*Cynodon dactylon*), which is grown for turf in the South and Southwest, is also a major cause of hay fever.

A Bad Host

Besides competing for light and other materials essential to growth, weeds can also make life tough for plants by playing host to insects and diseases that can infest desirable plants. In some cases, a pest requires both a specific weed and a specific crop to survive; get rid of the weed, and the pest is gone. For more information, see "A Host of Hosts."

Miscellaneous Weed Woes

Weeds can give any landscape a seedy, neglected look, reducing its property value. If your community has a mowing ordinance, you may even be fined if you allow tall weeds to grow on your property. At the very least, you'll create bad relations with your neighbors, who have to look at the weeds and deal with the seedlings that invade their yards and gardens.

In the vegetable garden, weeds compete with your crops for light, space, water, and nutrients.

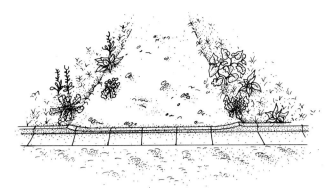

Weeds growing along paths and driveways can give your property a run-down, neglected look.

Weeds growing along roadsides—particularly near crossroads and driveway openings—can obstruct visibility and lead to automobile accidents. For all of these reasons, it's worth your time to deal with lawn and garden weeds before they get out of control.

A Host of Hosts

Some weeds are problems because they harbor harmful insects or diseases. If you control these weeds, you can reduce the risk of their associated problems attacking your garden plants. Below is a list of some common weeds and the pests or diseases they host.

Pepper grasses (*Lepidium* spp.) and tansy mustard (*Descurainia pinnata*) host diamondback moths, which feed on the leaves of cabbage-family plants.

Weeds in the nightshade (Solanaceae) family, such as horsenettle (*Solanum carolinense*) and black nightshade (*Solanum nigrum*), shelter insects that attack crops in the same family, like tomatoes, potatoes, and eggplant. Morning glories (*Ipomoea* spp.) house the sweet potato weevil.

Queen-Anne's-lace (*Daucus carota* var. *carota*) shelters carrot rust flies.

Pokeweed (*Phytolacca americana*) may be infected with cucumber mosaic, a viral disease that can spread to your cucumber crop.

In Praise of Weeds

It may be difficult to believe, especially if you've just spent a hot afternoon pulling quack grass out from around your roses, but weeds are not all bad. If the weeds seem to be winning, you may find consolation in some of the valuable services they provide, such as sheltering beneficial insects or protecting the soil from erosion.

Shelter for Good Bugs

"A Host of Hosts" on page 17 lists some weeds that shelter harmful insects while the pests aren't attacking your garden. But the insects that dwell in weeds aren't all harmful; in fact, some help your gardening efforts by being parasites on the pests!

Many beneficial insects spend part of their life cycle attacking pests and part feeding on pollen or nectar from flowers. Beneficials are often very tiny, so they prefer weeds with tiny flowers, such as members of the mustard (Cruciferae) or parsley (Umbelliferae) families. Weedy areas can also provide a haven for beneficials when you're cleaning up the garden after a harvest or at the end of the season.

Besides attracting beneficial insects, some weeds also provide habitat for butterflies. A few butterfly-attracting weeds include Queen-Anne's-lace (*Daucus carota* var. *carota*), wild asters (*Aster* spp.), milkweeds (*Asclepias* spp.), and goldenrods (*Solidago* spp.).

Erosion Control

No matter what kind of soil or growing conditions you have, there's always at least one weed that can adapt to your site. Weeds eagerly cover bare topsoil, which would otherwise wash away in the rain or blow away in the wind, leaving the less fertile subsoil.

In your garden, low-growing weeds like purslane (*Portulaca oleracea*) and scarlet pimpernel (*Anagallis arvensis*) can serve as a sort of "living mulch," covering the soil to keep it cool and to hold in moisture. Just make sure to pull these weeds as soon as they begin to flower, so they don't get the chance to go to seed and become pests.

Common purslane (*Portulaca oleracea*) can be useful as a living mulch in the vegetable garden. It's edible, too!

Barometers for Soil Health

Just as garden plants can have specific soil preferences, weeds are sometimes particularly well adapted to certain growing conditions. By looking at the kinds of weeds that grow in your yard and in your neighborhood, you can often get a clue about your soil's health and fertility. If red sorrel (*Rumex acetosella*) is common on your property, for instance, it's a good bet that your soil is acidic and poorly drained. For more information on how weeds can alert you to various soil conditions, see "Soil Clues from Weeds."

Wild Beauty

Some weeds can hold their own in a beauty contest against any pampered garden flower. In fact, some

Common yarrow (*Achillea millefolium*) thrives in well-drained, infertile soil. It can be attractive in a tough spot.

Asters come in many shapes, sizes, and colors. Some are weedy-looking; others make excellent garden plants.

weeds—or their better-bred relatives—are used as ornamentals. And many "weedy" plants are included in wildflower seed mixes because they become established and spread quickly. Asters (*Aster* spp.), goldenrods (*Solidago* spp.), black-eyed Susans (*Rudbeckia hirta*), and Queen-Anne's-lace (*Daucus carota* var. *carota*) are just a few of the colorful plants that some people consider weeds and others cherish as wildflowers.

Weeds for Eating

Through the years, people have found that some weeds are even edible and nutritious. Purslane (*Portulaca oleracea*) and lamb's-quarters (*Chenopodium album*) shoots are edible raw or cooked, and they are said to taste like spinach or chard. Cabbage-family weeds like garlic mustard (*Alliaria petiolata*) and shepherd's purse

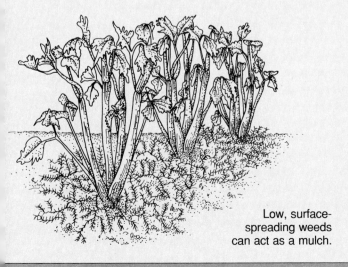

Low, surface-spreading weeds can act as a mulch.

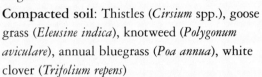

Soil Clues from Weeds

Your weeds can give you some hints about what kind of soil conditions you have. You'll get the most accurate picture if you take into consideration all of the weeds you have, not just one or two that might be flukes.

Compacted soil: Thistles (*Cirsium* spp.), goose grass (*Eleusine indica*), knotweed (*Polygonum aviculare*), annual bluegrass (*Poa annua*), white clover (*Trifolium repens*)

Sandy soil: Quack grass (*Agropyron repens*), puncture vine (*Tribulus terrestris*), horsetails (*Equisetum* spp.), red sorrel (*Rumex acetosella*)

Poor drainage: Buttercups (*Ranunculus* spp.), nutsedges (*Cyperus* spp.), plantains (*Plantago* spp.), barnyard grass (*Echinochloa crusgalli*), curly dock (*Rumex crispus*), ground ivy (*Glechoma hederacea*)

Infertile soil: Common yarrow (*Achillea millefolium*), thistles (*Cirsium* spp.), black medic (*Medicago lupulina*), crabgrasses (*Digitaria* spp.), plantains (*Plantago* spp.)

Fertile soil: Pigweeds (*Amaranthus* spp.), lamb's-quarters (*Chenopodium album*), foxtails (*Setaria* spp.), chickweeds (*Cerastium* spp.)

Acid soil: Red sorrel (*Rumex acetosella*), plantains (*Plantago* spp.), oxeye daisy (*Chrysanthemum leucanthemum*), many mosses

Alkaline soil: Shepherd's purse (*Capsella bursa-pastoris*), field pennycress (*Thlaspi arvense*), chicory (*Cichorium intybus*), mugwort (*Artemisia vulgaris*)

(*Capsella bursa-pastoris*) have a peppery flavor when raw and are also tasty when cooked. And don't forget the dandelion (*Taraxacum officinale*), whose young spring leaves are useful raw in salads or cooked as greens.

If you do decide to expand your horizons and try eating some of your weeds, you must make absolutely sure that you know what you are picking. There are some poisonous weeds that could be mistaken for edible ones. You'll also need to harvest the right part of the plant in the right season and be sure that the plant has not been sprayed with a pesticide. It's a good idea to take some kind of foraging workshop in your area to learn the guidelines for safe weed eating.

You can identify ground ivy (*Glechoma hederacea*) by its square, creeping stems, rounded leaves, and blue flowers.

Some weeds have distinctive flowers that make identification easy. This is common teasel (*Dipsacus fullonum*).

Knowing Your Weeds

The key to controlling weeds effectively is knowing what weeds you have. Once you know their names, you can find out all about their growth habits and choose the most appropriate control measures.

Getting Started

The "Guide to Weeds," starting on page 82, includes photographs and descriptions of most of the weeds you're likely to come across in your garden. If you have a weed you want to identify, flip through the pages and look for a photo showing a weed that resembles the one you have. Some weeds are so distinctive that it's easy to match them up with a picture. Others—like many grasses—are a bit more difficult to identify. In these cases, you'll want to read through the plant description below the photo to see if it fits your plant.

Detangling Weed Descriptions

If you need to use the descriptions to identify a particular weed, it helps to know what parts of the plant you should be looking at.

Flowers Weeds with flowers are usually the easiest to identify.

Look at the color and shape of the flower. Is it flat and daisy-like, trumpet-shaped, or tubular? Is the end of the flower smooth, or does it have puckered or scalloped "lips"?

You'll also want to notice where the flowers are and how they're arranged on the stem. Are they only at the top of the stem, or are they borne in the leaf axils (where the leaves meet the stem)? Some weeds have single flowers on separate stems; others produce rounded, spiky, or plumed clusters of many flowers.

Leaves After flowers, the next most obvious weed feature is the leaves. First, look at the shape of the leaf. It might be wide and round or long and narrow. Or it could be oval, triangular, heart-shaped, or kidney-shaped.

Clovers have three-leaflet leaves.

Next, check the surface and edge (margin) of the leaf. The leaf surface might be smooth, rough, waxy, hairy, mealy, or fuzzy. The edge can be smooth, toothed, wavy, or lobed with rounded indentations, like an oak leaf. Or it may be deeply divided with narrow, long indentations, like a fern leaf.

Some leaves are made up of many leaflets. For example, the leaf of both white clover (*Trifolium repens*) and poison ivy (*Toxicodendron radicans*) consists of three leaflets. Sometimes the leaflets are lined up in pairs along the leaf stem, so the whole leaf resembles a feather. In other cases, the leaflets are all attached to one central point, like fingers on a hand.

Now look to see how the leaves are arranged on the stem. Sometimes leaves attach in pairs at the same point on the stem,

Grasses can be difficult to tell apart.

which is called opposite. Some attach singly, with the next leaf attached farther up or down the stem, on the other side, which is called alternate. If more than two leaves come off of a single point on the stem, the arrangement is called whorled. Most leaves have a leaf stem, also called a petiole, that attaches the leaf to the main stem. Others attach directly to the stem.

Grassy weeds can look a lot alike, especially if they don't have a flower cluster (an inflorescence). One way to tell grasses apart is to look at the collar—the place where the upper surface of the leaf blade meets the stem. Some grasses have a membrane at the collar or a fringe of hairs—these are called a ligule. Some have a projection of tissue coming off the side of the collar—this is called an auricle. (You can identify quack grass because its auricle resembles a pair of clasping pointed arms.)

Flowers may form along the stems or at the tips.

Stems If you've looked at the flowers and leaves and you're still not sure about the identification, it's time to check the stems.

First, look at the stems' "posture." Do the stems stand straight and upright, or do they lie along the ground? Or do they do a little of both, first lying on the ground but turning upright toward the ends?

Next, see whether there is just one stem coming from the base of the plant or many. Does the stem (or stems) branch into smaller stems at some point, or does it stay single?

Other identification clues to look for include hairs, spines, or downy fuzz along the stem. Some stems may have ridges; a few even have spots.

The yellow blooms and toothed leaves of dandelions (*Taraxacum officinale*) are easy to recognize.

On some weeds, you may need to wait to see the fruit to find out exactly what you're dealing with.

Other Identification Ideas To help pin down the perfect match between a weed and a description, you may also want to look at features like fruit or roots. We usually think of fruit as being berries or the like, but the fruit is any structure in which the seeds develop. It may be a berry, but it may also be a pod, a puffy ball, or even a bur.

If you can, pull or dig the weed out of the soil so you can see the roots. Some weeds, like dandelions (*Taraxacum officinale*), form deep, thick taproots; grasses and other weeds grow from shallow, many-branched, fibrous roots. Particularly invasive weeds, like quack grass (*Agropyron repens*), also produce creeping roots or horizontal stems that spread over or through the soil and give rise to new plants.

If All Else Fails

Sometimes you may not be able to identify a particular weed that's plaguing your garden. Some weeds occur in such a specific habitat or localized area that they just don't show up in most field guides. If you need help to figure out a particular weed, take a sample of the whole weed—roots and all, if possible—to your local Cooperative Extension Service agent. Local arboreta, botanical gardens, and even garden centers may also be willing to identify the plant for you.

WEED CONTROL OPTIONS

There's something about weeds that makes normally rational people lose their heads. Weed-besieged gardeners either go into a weed-pulling frenzy or retreat into the house, draw the blinds, and hope the problem corrects itself. Neither of these approaches is the best plan: The frenzy leaves gardeners exhausted and is only a temporary solution, and retreating accomplishes nothing.

A more productive strategy for controlling weeds in your garden has three steps.

1. Identify the weed so you can find out how it spreads. Virtually all weeds can spread by seed; some also produce creeping stems or roots that can send up new plants. Use the photographic "Guide to Weeds," starting on page 82, and the tips covered in "Knowing Your Weeds" on page 20 to help you put a name on those troublesome pest plants. Then turn to "Plan a Weed Control Strategy" on page 24 to find out how different weeds have developed different ways to survive and spread.

2. Once you know how the weed spreads, pick a method for getting rid of it. This chapter covers many organic weed control options that you could use, depending on what weeds you have, where they are, and how much effort you want to put into removing

them. You may decide to control the weeds physically by pulling, hoeing, cutting, mowing, or blasting them with a torch. You'll find details on these options in "Take a Physical Approach" on page 26. "Bake Away Your Weeds" on page 30 tells how you can use the sun's heat for weed control. "Consider Biological Controls" on page 31 explains how animals can handle your weeds for you. Or follow the advice in "Choke Out Weeds with Smother Crops" on page 32, and let plants do the work. If all else fails, follow the advice in "Try Organic Herbicides" on page 33.

3. Finally, once the weeds are gone, take steps to keep them from coming back. "Keep Weeds Away" on page 34 and "The Mulch Miracle" on page 36 explain the various techniques you can use to prevent new weed problems, from managing mulch to wise watering and soil working. And if you decide that you don't need to eliminate all your weeds, check out "Turn Your Weeds into Wildflowers" on page 40 to learn how to live with them.

As you follow this three-step plan, you'll find that it soon becomes an automatic part of your garden maintenance. When you understand what problems you need to deal with and which techniques work best for you, you'll be on your way to safe, sane, and successful weed control in all parts of your yard and garden.

The weed control method you choose depends on which weeds you're dealing with and where they're growing. In flower gardens, for instance, hand-weeding and mulching are generally best.

Plan a Weed Control Strategy

To control your lawn and garden weeds effectively and efficiently, you need to use the right technique at the right time. This requires an essential piece of knowledge: How long do your particular weeds live? All plants have one of three life cycles: They can be annuals, biennials, or perennials. Knowing the life cycles of your weeds is your key to determining how they spread and how you can stop them.

To learn about your weeds' life cycles, you need to identify them first, with the help of the "Guide to Weeds," starting on page 82, and the tips covered in "Knowing Your Weeds" on page 20. Once you identify your weeds, you can find out their habits; this information is also included in the entries in the "Guide to Weeds." Then you can plan a strategy for hitting them when and where they are most vulnerable.

Annual Weeds Spread by Seed

Annual weeds, such as lamb's-quarters (*Chenopodium album*), live an entire life within 1 year; they sprout from seed, grow, flower, set seed, and die. Most annuals start this cycle in the spring and finish by fall. Winter annuals sprout in fall, grow a few inches tall, then go dormant until early spring. In spring, they resume growing and set seed by early- to mid-summer.

Mowing an area repeatedly until new sprouts stop forming can control both annual and biennial weeds.

Keep annual flowers from becoming weedy by pinching or cutting off the blooms before they produce seed.

Winter annuals, like common chickweed (*Stellaria media*), are the first weeds you'll see in the spring.

One part of controlling annuals is never letting them set seed. If the original plants die without making more seed, they won't come back the following year. Unfortunately, seeds from previous years' weeds can survive in the soil for many years, and new weed seeds may drift in on the wind or be carried in on clothing or fur. For these reasons, the other half of controlling annual weeds involves mulching and other techniques to prevent those existing seeds from sprouting.

Biennials Take 2 Years

For biennial weeds, such as Queen-Anne's-lace (*Daucus carota* var. *carota*), the seed-to-seed cycle spreads over 2 years. These weeds sprout from seed in the spring or summer, then usually grow into a ground-hugging circle of leaves called a rosette. The leaves produce sugars that move down to the roots and are stored as starch. The next spring, the plant uses the stored food energy to send up a flowering stalk, which may or may not have leaves. The plant flowers, sets seed, then dies.

You have two main options for controlling biennial weeds. You could dig out the rosette—root and all—the first year. Or, if the weed isn't too visible or crowding other plants, you could wait until the second year and cut the plant down to the ground. If you wait until the weed is just about to flower, the plant will have used up most of its stored energy and will likely not return.

Perennials Are Persistent

Wild garlic (*Allium vineale*), kudzu (*Pueraria lobata*), and other perennial weeds live for 3 years or more. Perennials, like biennials, store carbohydrates to fuel early growth the next spring. That food energy may be stored in a taproot, in spreading underground stems called rhizomes, or in spreading aboveground stems called runners or stolons. Or it may be in a tuber (like a potato) or a bulb (like an onion).

Loosestrife (*Lythrum* spp.) is tough to eliminate once it's established. Try digging out the perennial roots, or mow plants repeatedly in fall.

Some perennials, like dandelions (*Taraxacum officinale*), reproduce only sexually—by producing seed from fertilized flowers. But some also reproduce nonsexually, a process called vegetative reproduction. New plants can sprout from rhizomes and stolons. Tubers have "eyes" that produce new plants. And bulbs multiply, giving rise to new bulbs that can each become a plant. You can think of this vegetative reproduction as a type of self-cloning for plants.

bulb

Perennials are generally the most difficult weeds to control. The carbohydrates stored in their taproots, rhizomes, tubers, or bulbs give them a strong start each spring, as well as the power to grow again if their leaves are lost or damaged. Just preventing seed formation on perennials is not enough if you want to get rid of them; you need to either dig up all of the underground structures or force them to use up their food reserves by repeatedly removing their aboveground growth.

rhizome

Each time you remove a perennial's stems and leaves it draws on those stored carbohydrates to send up new growth. Because that new growth soon begins to photosynthesize more food for the plant, frequent weeding—every 7 to 14 days—is best. If you can't weed that often through the spring and summer, concentrate your weeding efforts before flowering and again later in the season. Perennials actively build up their food reserves in the late summer and fall to prepare for the next year's early growth. If you cut down the perennials several times during the fall, allowing a week or two of regrowth before you cut again, the roots may be too weakened to survive the winter.

tuber

If once-a-year weeding is the only option for a particular site, cutting weeds to the ground when the flower buds form is the best time. At that point, you'll weaken the roots, reducing the chance of them spreading farther. You'll also prevent the flowers from maturing and setting seed, reducing the chance of the plants coming back from seed.

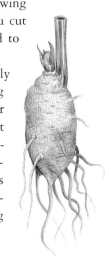

Take Out the Taproot

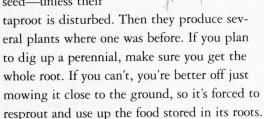

Some perennials, such as dandelions, usually only reproduce from seed—unless their taproot is disturbed. Then they produce several plants where one was before. If you plan to dig up a perennial, make sure you get the whole root. If you can't, you're better off just mowing it close to the ground, so it's forced to resprout and use up the food stored in its roots.

Take a Physical Approach

Weed control methods that involve pulling, cutting, or directly injuring weeds are called physical or mechanical controls. These methods are the most common because they are convenient and they work. The particular technique you'll use depends on how many weeds you have to control, how large an area they cover, and how much time you want to spend on them.

Pulling and Digging

These techniques are simple and effective for getting rid of a few weeds but are pretty tiring for large areas.

Pulling gets rid of annual weeds well, especially if the soil is damp enough that the roots come up. Just be sure not to toss weeds that reroot easily, such as purslane (*Portulaca oleracea*), on the ground. If you pull annual grasses, get as much of the roots as possible; the growing point of grasses is below the ground, and the plant might resprout if you just remove the aboveground portion.

Cape Cod weeder

Dutch scuffle hoe

Always try to pull annuals before they begin to flower and set seed. If they have already started flowering, collect the pulled weeds in a bucket; don't leave them on the ground, since their

Hoeing flower gardens once or twice early in the season can control weeds until your plants fill in to cover the soil.

seeds could still ripen and drop onto the soil.

Pulling doesn't work as well for perennials that reproduce with rhizomes, tubers, and bulbs because the food reserves are usually too deeply buried to pull up. Some, like dandelions (*Taraxacum officinale*), even sprout more plants if you break the top of the plant off the root.

Digging is a slightly better choice for perennials, assuming you get all of the buried portions. If you don't, these buried portions can produce new plants. Use hand tools to dig out small or shallow-rooted perennials. You may need a spading fork, spade, or shovel for tough, deep roots, like those of pokeweed (*Phytolacca americana*).

swan neck hoe

Hoeing and Tilling

When the weeds are too numerous to pull, a sharp hoe is a good solution. In most cases, hoes are best for young or annual weeds. But you can also deal a damaging blow to some established perennials—primarily those with thin or soft stems—by forcing them to use food reserves to replace the decapitated top growth.

pavement weeder

There are several schools of thought about the best

Digging can be time-consuming, but it's more effective than hand-pulling for getting rid of spreading perennials.

Pokeweeds (*Phytolacca* spp.) grow from deep taproots. To dig them out, you'll need a sturdy tool, such as a spade.

time to hoe. One says you should hoe when the soil is damp, so the roots pull out. Another says to hoe when the soil is dry, scraping the weed off at the soil surface without disturbing the soil and digging up new weed seed. Most of us just hoe when we find time and inspiration. All of these approaches are reasonable and certainly better than not hoeing at all, so use the one that works best for you. If you're trying to control perennial weeds, it's most important to hoe every 7 to 14 days to cut off the top growth before it starts sending food back down to the roots.

There are about a dozen styles of hoes, with assorted variations. Most you pull back toward you, holding the handle with your thumbs up and sliding the blade over the soil surface toward you, as if you were sweeping. If you use a hoe that you push, such as a scuffle hoe, hold the handle with your thumbs down, and push it in front of you like a snow shovel, with the blade just under the soil surface.

dandelion weeder

There are several types of hoes to choose from, including traditional hoes with a broad, straight blade, hoes with arrow-shaped blades that are

stirrup hoe

Neater Weeders

Ordinary hoes are traditional favorites for weeding vegetable gardens, but they aren't the last word in weeding tools. If you need a special tool for weeding in tight spots or if you just enjoy trying out handy garden gadgets, give some of the implements discussed below a try.

Pavement weeders are short-handled, with an angled, pointed blade used to scrape weeds growing between bricks or sections of sidewalk or in driveway cracks.

Dandelion weeders, also called asparagus knives or fishtail weeders, have a blade that resembles a forked tongue; the handle may be long or short. Use this tool to dig out grasses, small tree seedlings, or weeds with long taproots (such as curly dock [*Rumex crispus*]).

Cape Cod weeders and hot-bed weeders are short-handled, angled blades for cutting small weeds in tight places.

Hand cultivators have three claw-like tines for raking weeds from the soil; they may have short or long handles.

String trimmers can be powered by gas or electricity; high-powered models may have a blade attachment that can handle tough-stemmed weeds. Power trimmers are useful for quickly cutting weeds along fences and walls and for mowing small meadow areas. The drawbacks are their noise and the safety hazards they present.

Clippers, shears, and pruners are handy for cutting back vines and clump-forming weeds.

Mattocks and pick axes give the "umph" you need to dig out the roots of weedy woodies, such as shrubs and some vines.

good for digging out clumps of weeds, and hoes with circular blades that wiggle back and forth.

In most cases, though, the feel of the tool is more important than the particular blade that's attached. If you can, handle the tool before you buy it to see if the weight and balance feel comfortable. If the hoe feels heavy or awkward, you won't want to use it, no matter how great the blade is. For durability, look for a tool with a white ash or fiberglass handle joined to the metal with solid-socket or solid-strap construction.

If you have a large vegetable garden, with crops planted in rows, cultivating with a wheel hoe or rotary tiller may be more practical than with a handheld hoe. Shallow tilling—about 1 inch (2.5 cm) deep—can uproot young weeds without bringing too many buried seeds to the surface.

In almost all cases, it's best to avoid tilling perennial weeds with spreading roots, such as quack grass (*Agropyron repens*) and Canada thistle (*Cirsium arvense*). Even small pieces of chopped-up roots can sprout, multiplying your perennial weed problems. If you must rid an area of these weeds and can leave the spot unplanted for a growing season, you could try tilling the area shallowly every week or two until the root pieces stop sprouting new plants.

American pattern hoe

Mowing

Mowing doesn't get the roots, but it can keep all but the lowest-growing weeds from setting seed. And if you mow often enough (every week or two),

Thorough hand-weeding before planting will help get new gardens off to a weed-free start.

it weakens perennials by making them use up their food reserves to replace the top growth you removed.

Mowing works on woody shrubs and vines as long as the stems aren't too thick for the machine. For tall, tough weeds and tree seedlings no more than ¾ inch (18 mm) in diameter, use a heavy-duty string trimmer with a blade attachment. If you must control brush over a large area, consider renting a walk-behind tractor with a sickle bar attachment.

Fighting Weeds with Fire

Flaming is a weed control method that's used less often than it should be. Despite what it sounds like, flaming does not involve dousing your weeds with gasoline and tossing a match on them (tempting as that might sometimes be). Instead you use a propane torch with a fan tip or a special flaming tool designed for garden use.

Flaming has a few limitations that may account for its rarity. For one, it works best on weeds that are less than 2 inches (5 cm) tall; taller

Loosening the soil with a spading fork can make hand-pulling weeds a whole lot easier.

If weeds get out of control in paved areas, cut back the tops; then use fire or hot water to control regrowth.

annuals and established perennials may need repeated treatments. Flaming isn't much help for controlling woody vines and shrubs, since they are protected by their bark. This technique also is a fire hazard in dry areas or on mulches that catch fire easily, such as pine needles or sawdust.

When used carefully, however, flaming is a fast, easy, and effective way to control a variety of weeds. It is particularly useful for controlling weeds along fence lines and in sidewalks, driveways, patios, and other paved areas. It's also a great way to control

Whatever control you choose, use it before weeds set seed; otherwise, you'll have to deal with seedlings, too.

Getting into Hot Water

Who needs high-tech chemical sprays to get rid of pesky weeds? You certainly don't! If you can boil water, you have the power to create a simple but effective weed-killing spray. All you have to do is dump boiling water over the unwanted weeds, making sure it doesn't get on you or on plants you want to keep.

As with flaming, it may take several hours, or even a whole day, to see results. Boiling-water treatments work best on seedling weeds, since perennials would need repeated applications every week or two. It's not a practical way to manage large garden areas, but it's an easy alternative to flaming or hand weeding in sidewalks, patios, driveways, and other paved areas. If you do apply boiling water to garden weeds, be aware that it will take several weeks for the soil organism population to recover in the treated area. You may want to apply some compost to restock the beneficial organisms and supply extra nutrients for new plantings.

---

weeds when the soil is too wet to hoe, dig, or till.

Aim the flame at the top of the weed for a few seconds, hitting it with the invisible, hottest part of the flame outside the blue-white cone. The plant should not catch fire or even look scorched or wilted; in fact, you won't see any damage right away. The few moments of intense heat ruptures the plants' cells, the contents ooze out, and the plant gradually wilts and dies over the next several hours, up to 1 day later.

Pull out and compost the dead weeds, or flame them again to reduce them to ash. Treat established perennial weeds every week or two for several weeks to kill the regrowth. Gradually, even the toughest weeds should succumb.

Cut down tall weeds with a mower or string trimmer.

Bake Away Your Weeds

With the sun's heat and some plastic, you can destroy many of the weed seeds, stolons, rhizomes, tubers, and bulbs near the soil surface, greatly reducing the number of potential weeds. As a side benefit, you'll kill some disease-causing pathogens and soil-dwelling pests as well.

The process, called solarization, is simple: You cover bare soil with thick, clear plastic and let the sun bake it during part or all of the summer. Solarization is most effective against annual weeds, though it can kill or dramatically weaken even tough perennials like johnson grass (*Sorghum halepense*) and bermuda grass (*Cynodon dactylon*). It's a good way to convert a formerly grassy or weedy area into a vegetable, flower, or shrub bed, preventing the regrowth of many easy-to-miss shoots and seeds.

But although the process of solarization is simple, it definitely isn't fast. To get the maximum benefit, you need to leave the soil covered for at least 1 month and possibly as long as 3 months, depending on what kinds of weeds you want to control and where you live. Because the soil needs to be bare before you apply the plastic, you'll also have to hoe or pull any existing weeds, which can be a big job for large areas. For these reasons, solarization is usually reserved for serious weed problems that don't respond to less drastic solutions. But in the situations that warrant it, solarization is a tool without equal.

Step-by-step Solarization

Early- to mid-summer is the best time to lay out a solarizing setup. You can solarize a plot as small as 2 feet (60 cm) by 3 feet (90 cm). Or it can be as large as you want, as long as you have enough plastic to cover it. The site should be in full sun; otherwise, the soil may not heat sufficiently for good weed control. Once you've chosen the site, follow the steps here.

1. Prepare the soil by removing all weeds. Do any digging or tilling that you had planned before planting, then rake to remove any remaining plant debris, break up any big clods, and level the site. Dig a shallow trench around the area.

2. Moisten the soil thoroughly. (If the soil is sandy, lay a soaker hose over the area before going on to Step 3. Water every week during the process to keep the soil damp.)

3. Cover the soil with clear plastic sheeting at least 2 mil thick. (You can find the plastic at a hardware store.)

4. To anchor the plastic and seal the edges so heat won't escape, lay the edges in the trench surrounding the site and cover them with soil.

5. Now you wait. If any holes appear in the plastic, patch them with tape.

6. You can remove the plastic after 4 to 6 weeks if the weather has been hot and sunny. If the weather has been cool (around 75°F [24°C]) or cloudy, 8 to 12 weeks would be more effective.

After removing the plastic, give the soil a few days to dry before you plant. As much as possible, avoid stirring up the earth as you plant; the soil a few inches down will still contain weed seeds that could sprout if you bring them to the surface.

The heat of solarization will also kill some beneficial soil organisms, so the release of plant-available nutrients may be slower for several weeks. If plants in solarized soil are pale or grow slowly, apply a liquid fertilizer such as diluted seaweed or fish emulsion to provide nutrients in a readily available form. Mulching with compost can also help to restock the soil with beneficial organisms.

Solarizing Your Soil

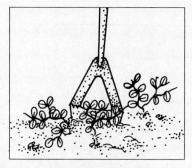
Remove existing weeds from the area you want to solarize.

Water the area to moisten the soil thoroughly.

Cover the site with a sheet of clear plastic; bury the edges.

Consider Biological Controls

The term biological control might make you think of mysterious, high-tech microorganisms that silently wipe out huge weed populations. But while specific fungi are occasionally used experimentally to control specific weeds on range lands, that technology is not yet available for the home garden. Nor are weed-eating insects, another area of research. So, when people talk about biological controls for weeds, they usually mean using plant-eating animals such as goats, geese, and rabbits—a much cuter, if less high-science, approach.

If you buy an animal for weed control, remember all of those things your parents said about animals being a big responsibility. Thoroughly look into what care

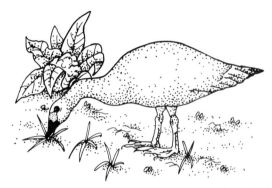

they need and how to manage them before buying. Check local ordinances to make sure you are permitted to keep animals in your yard. For more information, ask your local Cooperative Extension Service for literature and the names of local associations or breeders.

If you want to use animals to control weeds but don't want to buy and keep them, you may be able to work out a deal with someone who owns animals and is glad to have more grazing land. If you don't know animal owners, check classified newspaper ads placed by people selling animals and pitch your idea.

Whether you borrow or buy, you'll probably need to temporarily fence the area you want weeded, so the animals don't damage plants you want to keep. Here are a few other tips to consider if you'd like to use animals to control weed problems.

Goats Goats can clear a steep hillside better than any human or machine. Some people have found that Spanish or Angora goats are much more effective for clearing poison ivy (*Toxicodendron radicans*) and woody brush than common dairy goats. One or two goats are usually plenty for an acre or two.

Geese Geese are best for controlling grassy weeds, particularly in vegetable gardens (except chard, lettuce, and corn plantings!) and in orchards. All kinds of geese will work, though some growers prefer a breed known as White Chinese weeder geese. One or two geese are

Weed-killing Plants

Animals aren't the only living organisms that work for weed control—certain crops can help, too! Some plants produce toxins in their roots or leaves that make the soil inhospitable for other plants—a mechanism called allelopathy.

Some allelopathic species include annual ryegrass (*Lolium multiflorum*), oats (*Avena sativa*), wheat (*Triticum aestivum*), and winter rye (*Secale cereale*). These four make good smother crops; when you work them into the soil, their decomposing residues inhibit annual weeds. (See "Choke Out Weeds with Smother Crops" on page 32 for complete details about growing smother crops.)

Other plants that can help discourage weeds from sprouting include sweet potatoes (*Ipomoea batatas*) and sagebrush (*Artemisia tridentata*). These generally aren't practical as smother crops, but you could try growing them in one area of the garden and chopping the stem tips for use as mulch around transplants and established seedlings.

enough for most home gardens. It's best to start with youngsters—those at least 6 weeks old. Keep in mind that geese are very noisy, and they can be aggressive toward humans and other animals. They may also feed on your crops if they run out of other food; move them into new areas of the garden regularly.

Rabbits Rabbits may sound like unlikely candidates for garden weeding, but they can be useful if you manage them effectively. Build bottomless wood-and-chicken wire cages with removable roofs to contain the bunnies in the garden. A cage that covers about 1 square yard (1 sq m) is usually fine for one rabbit. Move the cage around the garden as needed as the weeds are eaten down. Young bunnies adapt to this system more quickly than older ones. Rabbits are usually quite effective for weeding around brambles, currants, squash, onions, and maturing corn; don't try them around peas, beans, lettuce, cabbage, broccoli, or carrots!

Choke Out Weeds with Smother Crops

With a little planning, you can even use plants to control troublesome weeds. Smother crops grow fast and close together, outcompeting the weeds for light and nutrients. They also enrich the soil when you turn them under before planting.

This technique is only useful where the site is bare (with no shrubs or desirable perennials). Try it in one part of the vegetable garden, rotating the site each year so all parts get treated every few years. Or use it to get a new site ready for a flower bed or shrub planting. It can even work for reclaiming overgrown ornamental plantings if you first remove the plants you want to save (set them in a nursery bed to grow until the bed is ready for replanting).

Once you've chosen the site, mow to cut down the largest weeds, then dig or till to prepare a seedbed for the smother crop. Scatter the seeds evenly over the surface, rake lightly, and tamp down the soil. Water with a sprinkler as needed to keep the soil moist until the seeds germinate. Mow the crop once or twice during the summer to prevent it (and any weeds) from flow-ering and setting seed. Till or dig in the smother crop in fall or the next spring. Wait at least a week or two before planting to give the plant residue a chance to break down in the soil.

Here's a rundown of some of the best smother crops:

- **Annual ryegrass** (*Lolium multiflorum*) germinates quickly, even in cool soils, but dormant seed may sprout for 2 or 3 years after and become a weed problem. Plant in the fall in the South and spring in the North at a rate of 1½ to 3 ounces (45 to 90 g) per 100 square feet (9.3 sq m).

- **Buckwheat** (*Fagopyrum esculentum*) matures in 2 months, so you can quickly smother summer weeds and still plant a fall garden. Plant 5 ounces (150 g) per 100 square feet (9.3 sq m) in the spring or summer. Buckwheat withstands heat well but not frost. It grows in most soils, including infertile and acid ones. Till or dig it in before or just as the plants bloom.

- **White clover** (*Trifolium repens*) is sometimes considered a lawn weed, but as a legume, it adds nitrogen to the soil as it smothers weeds. It's fast-spreading and tolerates shade, and it grows almost anywhere, except in deserts, hot tropics, and extremely cold regions. White clover is usually grown from one spring to the next. Before planting, apply a store-bought inoculant to the seed if white clover has never grown in the area. Sow ¼ ounce (7 g) per 100 square feet (9.3 sq m).

- **Winter rye** (*Secale cereale*) grows quickly in early spring and produces toxins that kill weed seedlings. Plant in well-drained soil in the late summer or fall at a rate of 4 ounces (120 g) per 100 square feet (9.3 sq m). Wait 3 to 5 weeks after turning it under in spring, then set out transplants or direct-sow large-seeded plants; small-seeded plants can't tolerate the toxins from freshly decomposed winter rye.

- **Winter wheat** (*Triticum aestivum*) competes against early weeds but won't interfere with spring planting as much as winter rye. Winter wheat prefers a fertile, loamy soil and a neutral pH. In late summer, plant 3 to 6 ounces (90 to 180 g) per 100 square feet. Dig or till plants under in spring.

Step-by-Step Guide to Growing a Smother Crop

Dig or till the planting area to prepare a seedbed.

Scatter the seeds of the smother crop over the soil.

Mow the crop once or twice during the growing season.

Dig or till the crop into the soil in fall or spring.

Try Organic Herbicides

Organic herbicides won't solve all of your weed woes, but they can be a useful alternative in certain situations. The herbicides that are acceptable to organic gardeners—basically soap, vinegar, and salt—all have one thing in common: They can kill any plant they touch (assuming you get enough of the material on the plant). In gardening lingo, these are called non-selective herbicides. For this reason, you must use them with caution to avoid damaging the plants you want to keep.

Soap-based Herbicides

If you've ever used soap sprays to control insect pests, you may have noticed the warnings that these sprays can injure some plants; you may have even seen the damage yourself. Herbicidal soap sprays take this damage one step further. They are formulated to break up the protective waxy covering on the leaves, causing the weeds to slowly dry up and die.

Herbicidal soap sprays work best on seedling weeds.

The soap works on contact—it isn't absorbed and moved through the plant—so you need to spray the entire plant thoroughly. It takes at least a few hours for the damage to show; the plant gradually turns brown.

Herbicidal soaps work best on young weeds that haven't had time to establish a good root system. Older annuals often grow back and usually require more than one application. Perennials with well-established food reserves can grow back so many times that, unless you want to run for the herbicide every week, it's probably easier to cut off the top growth until the food stores are depleted.

Vinegar and Salt

These two controls need to be used with even more caution than herbicidal soap because they can sterilize the soil for months. The first approach is to pour vinegar in the soil, making it too acid for plants to grow. The other is to pour salt on the soil and water it in, which kills the roots. For best results in either case,

Vinegar can make the soil too acid for weeds.

If you need to control weeds around desirable plants, you're better off hand-digging than using herbicides.

cut off or pull as much of the weed as you can before applying the control.

Because both of these substances have such a drastic effect on the soil, they are only appropriate where you want nothing else to grow, such as between the cracks in a sidewalk. Otherwise, consider less-toxic controls like flaming, dousing with boiling water, or pulling by hand.

Regular table salt will control many weeds.

Clean Up with Herbicidal Soap

Herbicidal soap can be a useful tool in your weed control strategy if you keep a few points in mind.

- Herbicidal soap can damage or kill any leaves or nonwoody stems it touches.
- Herbicidal soap is not labeled for use around vegetables.
- Seedlings that lack good root systems are easiest to control. You'll need to apply herbicidal soap more than once if you want to eliminate established annuals. Don't expect good control on perennials.
- Results are best if you apply herbicidal soap in warm, dry weather.
- It takes at least a few hours for the plant to begin turning brown.
- Wait 48 hours before planting in an area you've sprayed.

Keep Weeds Away

Getting rid of the weeds you have is just one part of an effective control program; the other key is keeping new weeds from getting started. Fortunately, there are many effective preventive measures you can use to make weed woes a thing of the past.

Minimizing Weed Imports

Although some weeds can travel on wind or animal fur, most stay pretty close to their parent plant. So once you get your weeds under control, they should stay that way—unless you inadvertently bring them in from the outside.

Here are things you can do to keep from spreading weeds from one place to another:

- If you've been working with a hoe, rake, spade, or other tool in a weedy area, clean the soil from the tool before you leave the area. While you're at it, clean off your shoes, too.
- Don't throw weed plants into the compost pile after they've flowered. And thoroughly compost all manure in a hot compost pile—one that you turn often as it heats up—before using it.
- When you buy seed, especially if it's in bulk (such as grass seed), read the label and pick the one with the lowest percentage of weed seeds.

Wipe or wash off tools after you use them to avoid carrying weed seeds from one part of the garden to another.

- Any time you sow seed, quickly scan the batch for seeds that don't match the rest and throw them out.
- When you buy plants in pots, check the soil surface for tiny weeds or evidence that weeds have recently been pulled from the soil, such as holes, loose soil, or parts of weed plants. If all of the pots are weedy or if some are clean but others hold weeds, shop elsewhere.
- If you live in a rural area where you draw irrigation water from a surface stream, add a filter to the irrigation system to catch weed seeds before they reach your garden.

Turning Up Trouble

Turning the soil seems like a lovely gardening tradition, so much so that many gardeners do it in the spring and again in the fall.

But for several reasons, turning the soil more than absolutely necessary is a bad idea. First, thousands of weed seeds lie dormant in the soil—often for years—waiting for conditions to be just right to grow. In many weed species, exposure to light can break that dormancy. When you turn the soil, you bring buried seeds to the surface, where they get the light they've waited for.

Another way you may turn up trouble is by tilling areas infested with perennial weeds that

---

Dig in the Dark

If you're determined to till but also want to keep weeds to a minimum, consider tilling your garden after dark. It may sound crazy, but researchers have had remarkable success with this technique, reducing weed cover by 70 to 80 percent. Apparently, exposure to just a few seconds of light is all some weeds need to germinate. If you till when it's dark, many of the seeds will be reburied without being triggered to sprout.

To try this for yourself, dig in any time between 1 hour after sunset to 1 hour before sunrise. Some researchers suggest eliminating all light that's visible to the human eye by using a military-type infrared scope with an infrared spotlight and only tilling on cloudy nights. Others claim that light from the moon or a lantern won't make a difference to the seeds, but it certainly will make things simpler for you!

have rhizomes or stolons, such as johnson grass (*Sorghum halepense*), quack grass (*Agropyron repens*), or Canada thistle (*Cirsium arvense*). A rotary tiller chops up those rhizomes and stolons into little bits, each one potentially capable of producing a plant, and soon you have a huge weed problem. Also, because most rotary tillers dig down into the soil, they can also bring up buried weed seed.

So how are you supposed to have a garden without digging? You could go a completely no-till route by covering the ground with some kind of mulch (like straw or black plastic) to smother the existing vegetation, then plant right through the mulch. Or you may just reduce the amount of digging or tilling you already do. In areas where you'd normally dig twice a year, just turn the soil in spring. If you use your tiller for weeding, set the blade to only go 1 inch (2.5 cm) deep so that you destroy the young weeds without bringing up much buried seed. For the ultimate in weed control, try the tip discussed in "Dig in the Dark."

Encouraging Healthy Competition

If you keep your plants healthy, they will be better able to compete with weeds—and insects and diseases, for that matter. Here are a few tips to keep in mind as you plan, plant, and maintain your garden.

- Choose plants adapted to your climate, soil, and amount of sunlight, so they'll be strong and vigorous.

Keeping your plants vigorous and spacing them properly will help them to cover the soil and discourage weeds.

Besides smothering existing weeds, mulches can prevent new weed seeds from getting a roothold in your soil.

- Don't set out transplants or sow seed too early in the year, or plants will get a slow start and be overtaken by weeds.
- Use the closest recommended plant spacing so plants can shade out lower-growing weeds.
- Add some form of organic fertilizer to the soil so plants get the nutrients they need.
- Water plants deeply when they need it; early signs of water deprivation include leaves that droop at midday and then perk up toward evening or that look duller than normal.

Anti-weed Watering

Have you noticed that during a dry spell, it seems that the only green plants are the weeds? Weeds often are better adapted than garden plants for scrounging scarce water resources from the soil. But you can level the playing field by seeing to it that you don't water the weeds when you water your plants.

That means, at the very least, letting the hose trickle at the base of plants, rather than watering from overhead with a sprinkler or handheld spray nozzle. Of course, if you have more than a half-dozen plants to water, moving the hose every 10 minutes becomes a real hassle. In that case, either well-placed soaker hoses or drip irrigation systems, which deliver water directly to the root zone without wetting the soil in between, is a worthwhile option.

Bark nuggets are rather coarse-looking, but they are long-lasting and useful in low-maintenance areas.

Compost works best when topped with a thin layer of a longer-lasting mulch, such as shredded bark.

The Mulch Miracle

Mulching is what is known in scientific lingo as an "elegant solution"—it's simple, but it works. All you do, in essence, is put something on top of the soil that covers up weed seeds and gets in the way of emerging weed plants. Either the seeds don't sprout at all, or the seedlings use up all of their energy and die before they reach the sunlight.

Even if it just helped to control weeds, mulch would be an important part of any garden. Happily, mulch offers many other benefits as well. It holds moisture in the soil, so you water less. It keeps soil cooler in the summer, so plant roots face less heat stress. In the winter, it keeps the ground frozen; this way, soils don't freeze and thaw repeatedly, heaving shallow-rooted plants out of the ground and leaving them on the soil surface to die. If you use a mulch that comes from a plant or animal, such as grass clippings or manure, it will also improve your soil by adding organic matter.

Unfortunately, mulch *can* have a few drawbacks. Slugs, cutworms, mice, and some other garden pests like to hide in it. And unless you keep it a few inches

away from plant stems, mulches can promote crown and stem rot. But if you select the right mulch for your conditions and manage it properly, you'll find that mulch is a valuable part of your weed control program.

Picking a Mulch

You have dozens of materials to choose from to use as mulch. Some are free and lying around your yard, like leaves and grass clippings. Others, such as bark chips and landscape fabric, require a trip to the garden center and an outlay of cash. Some, such as cocoa bean hulls, mushroom compost, and apple pomace, are products of local industries, making them inexpensive and easy to get in some areas and scarce in others.

With so many mulches to pick from, it can be hard to decide which to use. Part of your decision will depend on how much you want to spend and how available that particular mulch is in your area. The other part of the decision should be based on how you plan to use the mulch.

For weed control, bulky, chunky materials (such as bark nuggets) or thick barriers (such as cardboard and landscape fabric) do the best job of suppressing weeds. These are not necessarily the best materials for improving the soil because they break down slowly. So if you want your mulch to do more than smother weeds, you might have to combine a weed-smothering mulch with a fine-textured one that breaks down faster; put the coarse mulch on top of the fine one.

Fine-textured mulches like compost, manure, or grass clippings do a so-so job of keeping weeds down. They quell most annuals, but many perennials have enough energy to push through. And seeds that fall on top may find enough moisture and warmth to sprout and send their roots down through the mulch to the soil.

A few other factors you may want to consider when choosing a mulch are its appearance and its permanence. Coarse mulches like bark chunks may look fine around large trees but overwhelming in flower beds; straw is fine for the vegetable garden but too rough-looking for ornamental plantings. Coarse, heavy mulches tend to stay put and last for up to several seasons with minimal upkeep. Lighter mulches break down quickly, so they're a better choice in vegetable gardens and flower beds, where you turn the soil each year.

A Mulch Sampler

Almost anything that keeps light away from emerging plants can be a mulch, but there are some you're more likely to want in your garden than others. Here are tips on choosing and using a few of the most widely used mulches.

Bark Pieces Chunks, chips, and shreddings of bark are attractive, long-lasting mulches. The big chunks, sometimes called nuggets, are better than bark chips and shredded bark at discouraging weeds. Weed control is best when the bark is about 6 inches (15 cm) deep. If you're using it in garden beds, however, it's better to apply it only 3 to 4 inches (7.5 to 10 cm) deep; otherwise, you might also smother your desirable plants. Bark mulch is a little expensive, running about $3 for a bagged cubic yard. You'll pay less

A well-chosen mulch can accent your plantings as well as control your weed problems.

if you can find a source that sells it unbagged.

There are a few cautions you should keep in mind when considering and using bark mulches:

- Bags labeled "wood chips" can contain wood other than bark, including leftovers from the timber industry that might have been treated with chemicals that could harm plants.
- If you chip your own bark, let it sit outside for a few months before you use it to leach out any natural substances harmful to young plants. Turn the pile every few weeks to keep the chips from turning "sour."
- Cypress bark can be toxic to young, tender plants.
- Small chips and shredded bark can wash onto nearby sidewalks during a downpour, leading to more work keeping paths near mulched beds clean.

Organic mulches can break down over time. Add more each year to keep the soil or underlying mulches covered.

A 6- to 10-inch (15 to 25 cm) layer of straw makes an attractive-looking mulch for vegetables and fruit plantings.

Newspaper and Cardboard Mulches of cardboard or a thick layer of newspaper aren't especially attractive, but they are effective for smothering weeds. They create a barrier that even aggressive perennial weeds have a tough time breaking, but they still allow water to pass through.

Newspaper and cardboard are inexpensive and readily available. How thick the layer is and how rainy the season is affect how long these mulches last, but you can usually count on them to last one season. It's a good idea to cover them with another mulch to make them more attractive and to anchor them; at the very least, cover the edges with soil or a few rocks to keep them from blowing away.

Leaves Leaves make a good weed-suppressing mulch. You can shred them if you want a good-looking, fine-textured mulch or use them whole to form a dense mat. Apply either shredded or whole leaves in a 4- to 6-inch (10 to 15 cm) layer. If you're using leaves as a long-term mulch around perennials, trees, or shrubs, rake them off for a few weeks in the spring to let the soil warm up.

Landscape Fabric Good landscape fabric—also known as a weed barrier—can keep the areas under and around trees and shrubs nearly weed-free. For new plantings, spread these water-permeable sheets of spun or pressed plastic (now they also are made from wool!) on top of the soil; then cut holes or Xs to make room for the plants. In existing plantings, do your best to fit the fabrics around the base of the plants. Landscape fabrics can also be useful under decks, paths, and walkways; lay them before you build the deck or set the paving to prevent weeds from sprouting.

The barriers do have a few drawbacks. First, they're more expensive than most organic mulches. Also, they will eventually break down, so they have to be replaced

If you plan to use your compost as mulch, be especially sure you don't toss in any plants that have gone to seed.

every few years; exactly how long they last varies with the brand. Some fabrics are so loosely woven that they let weeds through. And in some cases, the roots of trees and shrubs grow through the fabric, making it tough to move or remove the mulch. You'll also need to cover the fabric with a layer of other mulch to make it look more attractive and to block sunlight, which can break the fabric down more quickly.

Plastic Sheeting Plastic, like landscape fabric, cardboard, and newspaper, is a tough barrier. Unlike those materials, however, plastic doesn't let water through. If you use it around plants in the vegetable garden, either punch little holes in it or run a soaker hose underneath so your plants will get the water they need. Or use plastic mulch where you want nothing to grow, such as under fences and along walks. When exposed to light, plastic becomes brittle and can rip and blow around; cover it with stones or another mulch to reduce these problems.

Old natural-fiber carpeting can be a useful mulch for paths or shrubs.

Compost makes a nutrient-rich mulch for all kinds of garden plants.

Straw makes a better mulch than hay, since it is usually seed-free.

Landscape fabrics make effective weedproof mulches. Lay them over prepared soil and cut slits for planting. Cover them with a layer of organic mulch.

Grass clippings look better when topped with a more attractive mulch.

Compost Compost is partially or completely decomposed yard waste and nonmeat kitchen scraps. While it makes a great soil amendment, it's only so-so at smothering weeds because it's usually fine-textured enough for weed seeds to grow in. For best results, apply a layer of compost under another mulch, like bark chips or shredded leaves.

Keep in mind that if you've thrown seedy plants (weeds, flowers—even rotting tomatoes) into the pile, you may end up spreading the seeds around your garden and creating a worse weed problem than before! Avoid throwing seeds into any pile, or save that compost for use as a soil amendment instead of as a mulch.

Hay and Straw Both hay and straw are loose mulches, so you have to apply a thick layer—6 to 10 inches (15 to 25 cm)—to get much weed control from them. Even then, tough perennial weeds that you missed before mulching can pop through, although they'll be weaker than normal. Straw is usually free of weed seeds, but hay might not be and can add to your weed problems.

Grass Clippings Grass clippings add organic matter to the soil, but you need to apply them deeply—about 6 inches (15 cm) of dry clippings or 1 inch (2.5 cm) of fresh clippings—to control annual weeds. Because clippings are lightweight and break down quickly, they aren't effective against most perennial weeds. Fresh grass clippings can mold and smell if you apply them too thickly; try mixing them with a dry mulch such as sawdust, shredded leaves, or bark chips. Avoid using clippings from lawns where the grass or weeds have gone to seed and from lawns that have been treated with pesticides or herbicides.

Pine Needles Pine needles, also called pine straw, are used widely in the southern United States. They last for a long time (up to several seasons) and increase soil acidity (a real plus for acid-loving plants like blueberries, azaleas, and camellias). But, like grass clippings, pine needles are too loose to keep down perennial weeds. And the needles are a fire hazard during droughts. Don't collect them from the forest; leave that organic matter to fertilize the trees. Apply a 6-inch (15 cm) layer.

Managing Your Mulch

There are a few simple things to keep in mind about when to apply mulch. First, you'll get the best results if you mulch bare soil—that means before the weeds start growing or right after you hoe, cut, or pull weeds that have already come up. Also make sure the soil is moist (but not soggy) before you mulch.

Also be aware that mulch can thwart desirable seedlings as well as weed seedlings. If you're growing flowers or vegetables from direct-sown seed or if you're depending on self-sown seedlings from last year's plants, wait until the seedlings are about 4 to 6 inches (10 to 15 cm) tall before mulching. An added benefit of waiting is that bare soil warms up more quickly in the spring than mulched soil, so your seedlings will get off to a better start.

Turn Your Weeds into Wildflowers

With today's growing appreciation for the environment, a more natural landscaping style is becoming accepted in all but the most conservative neighborhoods. Wildflower meadows, butterfly gardens, restored prairies, and mini-wildlife habitats are replacing formal flower gardens and lawns. These low-maintenance areas are terrific time-savers, especially for gardeners with large lots.

Low-maintenance areas welcome many beautiful and useful "weeds," but they require some watchfulness on your part to keep out invasive and undesirable ones. If nasty weeds take hold in a natural planting, they can be a pain to control, since you can't mow often or mulch.

Before you start a meadow garden in your backyard, it's important to discuss your ideas with your neighbors. If you simply stop mowing and let the grass grow, you may be dealing with complaints instead of compliments on your new natural area. If you explain your intention, people may be more apt to view the area as a garden than as an eyesore. Keeping a strip of mowed turf around the area helps to give the impression that the area is intentional.

In out-of-the-way areas, you may decide to create a meadow garden, where weedy wildflowers aren't a problem.

Starting Clean

A natural planting is easiest to manage if you start with a weed-free area. Almost any of the methods covered in this chapter will do for a small area. If you have a lot of ground to clean up, consider solarizing it or burying it in a deep (6- to 8-inch [15 to 20 cm]) mulch. Use a fine-textured mulch that decomposes quickly—such as compost or well-chopped leaves—so you won't have to rake it off to plant. Mulch has the added advantage of improving the soil.

Grooming the Weed Patch

Even natural areas need a little care to keep them from getting out of hand. To keep woody vines, brush, and tree saplings from taking over, cut your meadow back to 6 to 10 inches (15 to 25 cm) in late fall or early spring. A lawn mower will work, if you can set yours high enough. Alternatives to the mower include various swashbuckling blades, such as machetes, scythes, serrated weed cutters (also called yo-yos), and grass hooks. A good gardening equipment catalog or hardware store will carry all sorts of nifty cutting tools. String trimmers are a possibility, but they may not be able to cut the woodiest stems; you'd have to cut the remainders by hand.

Fleabanes (*Erigeron* spp.) are great for easy-care mid-summer color in informal gardens and meadow plantings.

If you are converting a lawn to a wildflower meadow, you may not have to start with bare soil. The approach you take depends on the kind of grass you have. Most Northern grasses, such as Kentucky bluegrass and red fescue, aren't terribly aggressive, so you may decide to leave the lawn grass and overseed with wildflower seed. Just mow the lawn as short as you can in early fall, use a metal rake to rough up the soil a little, and scatter the seed thickly. Both the grass and the flowers will grow in spring. The grass will protect the soil while the wildflowers are getting established and while they are dormant in winter. And since you haven't had to expose or stir up the soil, there's less chance of unwanted weeds getting started.

If you have an aggressive Southern grass, such as bermuda grass or St. Augustine grass, get rid of it before you plant wildflower seed. Try one of these methods:

- Mow the lawn as short as possible, then cover it with black plastic for about 2 months in summer to block out light and water. When the grass is yellow and clearly dead, uncover the area and sow your wildflower seed. The dead grass will act as a mulch for the germinating flower seeds.
- Till the lawn, then rake up all of the grass tops and creeping roots so they don't resprout.
- Strip off as much of the grass as you can with a spade or a rented sod-cutting machine; then dig out any remaining roots.

Solarizing after any of these treatments will help you be doubly sure that the grass is dead.

Besides being beautiful and low-maintenance, meadows are an ideal habitat for bees and butterflies.

From Bad Weeds to Good

If you have a natural planting full of weeds you don't like and you want to shift it to weeds you do like, play Mother Nature and use your subtle influence to discourage the bad weeds and encourage the good. Here are some tricks to try:

- Change the soil conditions away from what the bad weeds like and toward what the "good" weeds like. This may mean changing the pH by liming or adding sulfur, watering, or loosening compacted soil. This approach is kind of a long shot, since new "bad" weeds may appear on the site. But if you have a particularly pesky weed like red sorrel (*Rumex acetosella*), you may be able to discourage it and make room for more desirable plants.
- Keep bad weeds from spreading. You can pull them up or cut them back before they flower. Perennial weeds will require repeated cutting— every week or two—to weaken them.
- Encourage good weeds by letting them self-sow or by collecting their seed (wait until it turns brown) and scattering it about. You can also buy wildflower seed and sprinkle that over the area.

In a garden setting, some weeds—such as chicory (*Cichorium intybus*)—can actually make attractive plants.

WEEDS IN THE VEGETABLE GARDEN

When it comes to controlling weeds in your vegetable garden, there's good news and bad news. The bad news is that vegetable gardens usually have areas where the soil is bare and exposed to light, so they are open invitations to weed growth. The good news is that you can start your vegetable garden over each year, so keeping weeds from invading and taking over is usually no big deal.

Most of the time, the weeds that spring up in vegetable gardens are annual weeds, those that grow only from seed and live one season. You can, within a few years, reduce the number of annual weeds to nearly nothing by keeping those weeds from going to seed and by mulching to smother weed seeds hiding in the soil.

Perennial weeds—those that return year after year and have a food-storing structure such as a taproot or rhizomes—are less common in vegetable gardens because the soil is usually turned each year. But perennials can be a problem if brambles, thistles, or some other perennial used to grow where your vegetable garden is now. Perennial weeds *can* also creep in from areas adjacent to the vegetable garden, such as lawns.

In this chapter, you'll learn an array of approaches to preventing weeds, many of which you can use early in the season, before summer's heat saps your interest in the garden. In "Stopping Weeds before They Start" on page 44, you'll learn how to keep weeds from getting a foothold in a new garden, which mulches work best for weed control, and how to water your vegetables, not your weeds.

To produce a bountiful harvest for you, your plants need all the light, water, and nutrients they can grab. For that reason, be diligent about getting rid of any weeds that do manage to take root. Hoeing and pulling work most of the time. But if for some reason you have a heavy infestation, "Controlling Vegetable Garden Weeds" on page 48 suggests ways to get it under control. "Fighting Weeds in Fruit Plantings" on page 50 offers special tips for weed control around strawberries, berry bushes, and fruit trees.

Finally, if you're *really* interested in taking a bite out of your weed problem, "Eating Your Weeds" on page 51 includes a list of edible weeds and suggestions for how to use them.

Vegetable gardens are prime sites for weed problems, since there's usually lots of space for the weeds to pop up between plants. Use mulches to minimize weed seedlings and hoeing or hand-pulling to control the rest.

Stopping Weeds before They Start

In the vegetable garden, a few minutes of prevention are worth hours of cure. There are several ways to keep weeds from getting started.

Let Sleeping Weed Seeds Lie

The traditional practice for preparing the soil has been to dig it up each spring and fall, turning it to a depth of about 8 inches (20 cm). But many gardeners now opt to turn their soil only once a year. One excellent reason to cut down on cultivation is that hundreds of weed seeds sleep buried in the soil, just waiting for some natural or artificial event to lift them up near the light, moisture, and oxygen they need to grow. So by disturbing the soil less, you uncover fewer weed seeds.

Still, you do need to prepare your soil to some extent for planting. The right method for you depends on your soil. If your soil is loose and sandy, try just digging a hole for individual plants. If the soil is heavy and clayey, try turning it in the fall with a spading fork (this is also a good time to add organic matter such as compost), then raking the surface in the spring to break up large soil clods before you plant.

There is one case where more frequent soil turning may be useful: if your vegetable garden has a heavy infestation of perennial weeds. Turning the soil twice a year—by hand, not with a rotary tiller—can help to keep perennials in check by disturbing their food-storage structures and bringing them to the surface to dry out. Unlike digging by hand, a single pass over perennial

Rising Above Weeds

You can literally cover up much of your weed problem by building raised beds for your vegetable garden. Side benefits include better drainage, often better soil, and a deep, rock-free rooting area for your crops.

To start, closely mow the area where the raised bed will be, then use boards, cinder blocks, or untreated landscape timbers to build walls that are at least 6 inches (15 cm) high. Make the bed 3 to 5 feet (90 to 150 cm) wide so you can reach in from each side without stepping in the bed; it can be any length you want.

Fill the walled-in bed with a mix of soil and compost. To make sure the bed is weed-free, you may want to solarize it before planting; see "Bake Away Your Weeds" on page 30 for instructions.

Mulch raised beds to prevent new weeds from gaining a foothold as well as to conserve water; raised beds drain faster and require more watering than ground-level plantings, especially in hot or dry regions.

weeds with a rotary tiller can actually make your weed problem worse because it chops and spreads rhizomes, tubers, and stolons. If you do want to till where there are perennial weeds, be prepared to till again every week or two until new sprouts no longer emerge. Then go back to once-a-season tilling or digging.

Three Ways to Turn a Lawn into a Vegetable Garden

Use a spade to remove the sod. Slip the blade just under the surface to cut the roots.

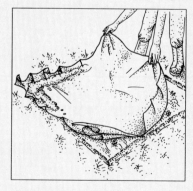

Solarize the area by covering it with clear plastic for several months during the summer.

Mulch the area thickly. It may take a month or two to completely smother the grass.

Mulch your vegetables to cover the soil until plants fill in.

Getting rid of as many weeds as possible before you plant your garden will make later control easier and let your crops get off to a good start.

A Shady Scheme

You can keep weeds from getting the light they need to sprout and grow by planting your vegetable crops close enough together to shade out the weeds.

The quickest way to get the garden to fill in is to grow vegetables from the largest transplants you can find. But even if you grow vegetables from small transplants or from seed, you can still take advantage of shade. If you're planting in rows, set out your seeds or plants at the closest recommended spacing on the seed packet or plant label. Or experiment with a more intensive gardening method by staggering plants in beds or wide rows rather than using straight single rows.

While you're waiting for your vegetable plants to get big enough to shade out weeds, use other weed control methods, such as hoeing or pulling. Mulching is a good idea, but wait until seedlings are 4 to 6 inches

(10 to 15 cm) tall, and keep the mulch at least 2 inches (5 cm) away from the stems to prevent stem rot.

Good Mulches for Vegetables

If you don't have many weeds, almost any mulch will do. Grass clippings, shredded leaves, and straw are popular because they smother weeds that aren't overly vigorous, and they break down into materials that feed the plants and improve the soil. If you have

Clearing the Land

If you're starting a brand-new vegetable garden, odds are that you'll have to clear away some lawn to make room for it. To keep the ghosts of the grass from rising among your vegetables, make sure the lawn is gone for good.

First, get rid of the grass. One way is to dig it up, including the roots (shake the topsoil from the roots back into the garden). Or cover the area with black plastic, cardboard, old carpet, or a thick layer of newspapers until the lawn yellows and dies; that could take a month or two. Another alternative is to mow the grass short, till the area, and rake out all of the roots and runners.

If you can wait a few summer months to plant, solarize the bare soil to kill weed seeds and any grass that remains. For instructions, see "Bake Away Your Weeds" on page 30.

a serious weed problem, especially with tenacious perennial weeds such as quack grass (*Agropyron repens*), you need a stronger mulch. The ideal mulches for this purpose are those that form a solid barrier and either break down or can be removed at the end of the year. Good choices are newspaper, cardboard, aluminum foil, or black plastic.

Water penetrates newspaper and cardboard; it doesn't penetrate aluminum foil or black plastic, so if you use these, you'll need to run a soaker hose or drip irrigation system under them. Black plastic also helps to warm the soil, so it's a good choice for mulching early-spring plantings and heat-loving summer crops like melons. If you use plastic to mulch around lettuce, spinach, and other cool-season crops into the summer, cover it with a lighter mulch like straw to keep the soil from getting too warm. Besides suppressing weeds, aluminum foil mulches

A thick layer of straw makes an attractive and effective weed-suppressing mulch for vegetable gardens.

can confuse aphids (tiny plant-feeding pests) and prevent them from landing on your crops.

You can lay these mulches on the soil either before or after planting. If you apply them before planting—usually the easiest option—you'll need to cut holes for transplants and slits for seeds. Before you lay out the barrier mulch, add a nutrient-rich mulch to the soil, such as compost or well-rotted manure, or scatter a commercially available dry organic fertilizer according to package directions.

At the end of the year, remove aluminum foil and

From Friend to Foe

As if the usual array of weeds wasn't enough, even the vegetables you pamper one year can turn on you the next. The seeds of that ripe tomato that fell to the ground unnoticed can sprout the next year, sending up unwanted plants in your carrot bed; the fallen kernels of sweet corn may pop up in your peppers.

These unwanted reminders of last year's crop in that spot are called volunteers. Besides tomatoes and sweet corn, cucumbers and squash are notorious for popping up where they're not wanted.

The best way to prevent volunteers is to pick up all fallen fruit and toss it into the compost pile. There, they'll either sprout and then die when you turn the pile or be killed by the heat an active compost pile generates. If you don't turn your compost pile regularly or if it doesn't feel hot soon after it's built, the seeds may survive in your pile. In that case, save that compost for mixing into the soil before planting or use it under another mulch, rather than as a surface mulch.

Aluminum foil mulches prevent weed seeds from germinating and can help to keep aphids off your plants.

Mulch thinly around seedlings to avoid smothering them.

Setting your plants at slightly closer-than-normal spacing will encourage them to fill in quickly, leaving no room for weeds.

black plastic. If the materials are still in good shape, you can use them the next season. Remove any of the newspaper or cardboard that has not broken down, and add it to your compost pile or dig it into the soil. For more about selecting and managing mulches, see "The Mulch Miracle" on page 36.

Wise Watering

It's a given that you'll need to water your vegetables sometime during the growing season, since even normally rainy climates can have dry spells during the summer. Rather than sprinkling the whole garden, giving a drink to vegetables and weeds alike, you can water in ways that discriminate against weeds (and save water, too).

One way is to snake a soaker hose through the garden so it rests near the base of your vegetable plants. A soaker hose is covered with bumpy pores that "sweat," slowly soaking the soil. Most of the water will moisten the soil near the vegetables' roots, leaving the weeds in the rows to parch in the sun. Of course, any weeds that lie in the hose's path will get a drink. So when you weed, be sure to check those spots.

A drip irrigation system is more precise than a soaker hose because it delivers water only

to the plants you want. Drip irrigation systems are made up of a network of plastic tubing; each plant has its own skinny tube delivering water to its roots. Drip irrigation systems are more of an investment than a soaker hose and require more planning and upkeep to work well, but they are a tremendously convenient and efficient way to water.

Drip irrigation waters your plants, not the weeds.

Postpone Planting to Wait for Weeds

One rather sneaky but effective weed control method is known as the "stale seedbed" technique. In this case, you prepare your soil as normal, but instead of planting, you water the soil and wait for the weeds. Give them a week or two to sprout, then get in there and flame them, scrape them from the surface with a hoe, or till shallowly (about 1 inch [2.5 cm] deep) to destroy the shoots before you plant. Repeating the procedure once or twice more will give the best results, but even one treatment will help your crops get the jump on the remaining weed seeds.

Controlling Vegetable Garden Weeds

While prevention can go a long way toward reducing vegetable garden weeds, it's probable that a few weeds will pop up somewhere during the season. When weeds do sneak past your defenses, you have several ways to get rid of them.

Hand-pulling and Hoeing

When it comes to killing weeds that have cropped up among your crops, the tried-and-true methods are pulling them out by hand or hacking them down with some type of blade (usually a hoe). You can also try flaming them, if you take care not to damage the vegetable plants nearby. For details, see "Take a Physical Approach" on page 26.

Whichever method you choose, don't be fooled into thinking one weeding will get you through the season. The secret to fast and easy weed control is persistence. Take a little time each week to walk through the garden, and be ready to pull, cut, torch, or spray the weeds that have come up since the last time. You'll kill annuals as they emerge and weaken perennials by forcing them to use up food stores to regrow. And no weed will get the chance to set seed. Best of all, you'll use less time and energy weeding a little each week than you would if you waited until the weeds were a tall, menacing, seed-filled mess.

An edging strip is a good way to keep lawn grasses from creeping into your vegetable plantings.

It's easy to pull weed seedlings from moist soil.

Smothering Weeds

Weeds like the same things as your vegetables: light, water, and nutrients. If you're willing to leave part of the garden unplanted for a season, you can deprive the weeds of all three with a smother crop.

A smother crop is a plant that grows well when crowded. By growing close together, smother crops choke out weeds. Many smother crops—including winter rye (*Secale cereale*) and annual rye (*Lolium multiflorum*)—are grasses; some broad-leaved plants, like buckwheat (*Fagopyrum esculentum*), are also effective.

Since the objective of a vegetable garden is to produce vegetables, the smother crop needs to do its work either before or after the vegetable-growing season. A smother crop

Hoeing is easiest when weeds are still small and tender.

Hand-digging is helpful for controlling deep-rooted weeds.

A cover crop acts as a "living mulch" to crowd out weeds.

A tidy, well-maintained, weed-free vegetable garden is a pleasure to look at as well as a treat to harvest from.

Field bindweed (*Convolvulus arvensis*) is a particularly pesky weed along fence lines.

of a winter annual grass such as winter wheat (*Triticum aestivum*) covers the soil in the fall as well as in the early spring, but you can turn it under early enough for it to break down (2 to 4 weeks before you plan to plant).

If you have an infestation of truly horrible weeds—such as Canada thistle (*Cirsium arvense*) or quack grass (*Agropyron repens*)—you'll need to take the vegetable garden out of production for a year to let the smother crop do its job. You can plant buckwheat in the spring, turn it under before it goes to seed, then follow it with another buckwheat crop in the summer and winter wheat in the fall. For more information on selecting smother crops, see "Choke Out Weeds with Smother Crops" on page 32.

Handling Problem Spots

Weeds can be especially problematic at the edges of the vegetable garden. The grass may creep in from the lawn, and a variety of weeds—especially twining ones like field bindweed (*Convolvulus arvensis*) or morning glories (*Ipomoea* spp.)—may lurk along the fence.

To keep the lawn from encroaching, use a barrier such as an edging strip that gives 2 to 3 inches (5 to 7.5 cm) of protection both above *and* below the ground. A flat mowing strip also helps. To make one, lay a band of bricks or paving stones along the edge of the garden, so their surface is even with or just slightly above the ground. When you mow, let the wheels on one side of the mower ride on the strip so you can trim right up to the edge of the lawn.

If your vegetable garden backs onto a fence, try to resist the urge to plant right against the fence. (This may be difficult, since fences are such a great ready-made support for cucumbers and other climbing crops.) At the very least, use a mulch along the fence that creates a strong barrier, such as black plastic or cardboard. Check the fence regularly for invading weeds, and hand-pull any that appear.

If your vegetable garden is along a fence, mulch along the base of the fence to keep weeds from creeping in.

Fighting Weeds in Fruit Plantings

Unlike a vegetable garden, which you replant each year, fruit plantings tend to be relatively permanent. For that reason, make sure the area is as free of weeds and weed seeds as possible before you plant. If time allows, solarize the soil (as explained in "Bake Away Your Weeds" on page 30) or grow a smother crop (see "Choke Out Weeds with Smother Crops" on page 32) before planting.

Strawberries

Strawberries send out runners to produce new plants, so any mulch you use must be sparse enough to let the runners reach the soil. Straw is a popular choice; so are pine needles. Spread the mulch about 1 inch (2.5 cm) thick. Pull out any weeds that emerge through the mulch. Add another 1 or 2 inches (2.5 to 5 cm) of mulch in the fall to protect the plants during the winter.

Berry Bushes and Brambles

A hoe and about 4 inches (20 cm) of mulch are your best tools for keeping down weeds around blueberries, currants, gooseberries, and brambles (such as raspberries and blackberries). You'll especially appreciate the long handle on your hoe if you grow bramble cultivars with thorns. Training brambles to a post-and-wire trellis will also help to keep the plants under control for easier weeding.

Rabbits are an alternative for controlling weeds

Controlling brambles with trellises makes weeding much easier.

around brambles. Contain each rabbit in a screened, bottomless frame that is 1 yard (1 m) long on each side, and move the frame as the rabbit finishes each area. Remove rabbits from the berry patch a few hours before sunset to keep them from burrowing out of their temporary pen. Young rabbits adapt to this weeding arrangement more readily than adults.

Fruit Trees

It's likely that your fruit trees are already surrounded by one of the best weed control materials: grass. Even commercial orchards have returned to growing grass between the rows of trees because it stops soil from washing or blowing away and competes well against weeds.

To make maintenance easier, however, it's best to remove the grass in a 2-foot (60 cm) ring around the base of each tree. (That will make mowing simpler and reduce the chance of damaging the trunk with the mower.) Mulch the bare area with a 6-inch (15 cm) layer of straw, compost, pine needles, or other organic mulch. Rake the mulch away from the trunk in fall to keep rodents from nesting in it and feeding on the tree bark.

Rabbits can be handy for weeding around fruit plantings. Make a frame to keep the animals where you want them.

Besides keeping weeds down, mulching around your strawberries will prevent the fruits from resting on the soil.

Sunflowers can be weedy, but they are still popular garden plants for their colorful flowers and tasty seeds.

Candied or fresh, the delicate flowers of sweet violets add a charming touch to desserts and salads.

Eating Your Weeds

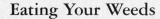

If you can't beat 'em, eat 'em! Many weeds are surprisingly tasty in salads or as cooked greens. In fact, some weeds, including dandelion (*Taraxacum officinale*) and purslane (*Portulaca oleracea*), are sometimes grown on purpose for their edible parts. Even if you don't want to encourage weeds for eating, you may want to make use of the ones you already have.

In most cases, you should harvest weeds while they are young and tender, just as you would other greens. And, of course, you should make sure you know exactly what you're picking before you eat it. To help you identify unknown plants, the "Guide to Weeds," starting on page 82, offers photos and descriptions of 140 common weeds. If you aren't absolutely sure of the identity or edibility of a particular weed, ask your local Cooperative Extension Service or a foraging expert in your area before you eat it!

A Sampler of Edible Weeds

Here are some tips on picking and preparing several common edible weeds.

Black Mustard The fresh young leaves, flowers, and newly formed seedpods of black mustard (*Brassica nigra*) lend a mustardy tang to salads. You can also make mustard from the dried, ground seeds. To collect the seeds, cut the plant at the ground after the seedpods turn brown but before they open. Hang the plants upside down in a brown paper bag to catch the seeds that fall. Rub the seeds through a sieve to remove the chaff; wear rubber gloves to avoid the irritating oils.

Common Lamb's-quarters Use small, tender leaves of common lamb's-quarters (*Chenopodium album*) in salads, or lightly steam them to use as greens.

Dandelion Use the tender young leaves fresh in salads or cooked as greens. And, of course, there's always dandelion wine.

Purslane Raw or cooked, the succulent leaves and stems of this lowly weed are tasty and nutritious. Use the fresh shoot tips to add a tart crunch to salads; steam any of the aboveground parts or use them to thicken soups.

Queen-Anne's-lace Dig up the taproot of Queen-Anne's-lace (*Daucus carota* var. *carota*) in fall and use it as you would garden carrots. Keep in mind that this wild version may be woodier and less sweet than cultivated carrots.

Shepherd's Purse To pepper up salads, soups, and stews, add just a few of the leaves and flowers of shepherd's purse (*Capsella bursa-pastoris*).

Sunflower Sunflower (*Helianthus annuus*) seeds are a traditional snack food. Wait until the seeds have hardened in the seed head. Then cut the stem off about 6 inches (15 cm) below the seed head and hang it indoors, upside down, in a paper bag. Once the seeds fall from the flower head, eat them fresh or roast them.

Sweet Violet The strongly sweet flowers of sweet violet (*Viola odorata*) can be candied for desserts or used fresh in fruit salads.

WEEDS IN ORNAMENTAL PLANTINGS

One of the obvious purposes of an ornamental plant—a flower, vine, shrub, or tree—is to add beauty to the landscape. Maybe that's why weeds really stick out in ornamental plantings—their unattractive, messy growth habit contrasts so sharply with the beauty of flowers and the tidiness of shrubs and trees.

If weeds were just messy-looking, that might not be so terrible, but the problems don't stop there. Weeds can rob flowering plants and newly planted shrubs, vines, and trees of the water and nutrients they need to thrive. (Established trees and shrubs can hold their own against most weeds—except weedy vines that twist around them and choke their trunks and branches.)

You don't have to put up with weeds in your landscape. In this chapter, you'll find out you can get rid of the weeds you have and, more important, prevent new weeds from ever getting started. You'll learn how to clean up weeds, then use mulching and other methods to keep them from coming back. In "Weeds in Your Flowers" on page 54, you'll also learn how to prepare and plant new flower beds to discourage weeds. "Stopping Weeds under Trees and Shrubs" on page 60 covers tips for weed control around these permanent plantings.

Sometimes the plants we grow as ornamentals perform so well that they actually become weeds themselves. They may spread so aggressively that they grow where we don't want them, crowding out less pushy plants. Or they may have messy habits, like dropping twigs and squishy fruit. These aggressors present a challenge, since the traits that make them compete so well can also make them hard to control. In some cases—especially with weedy trees—the answer may be to find a way to coexist with a plant rather than to get rid of it. "When Good Plants Turn Bad" on page 58 and "Coping with Woody Weeds" on page 62 explain how flowers, shrubs, and trees can become weeds and point to some common culprits. These sections also offer suggestions for getting rid of the pesky plants or at least bringing them under control.

When you've put time and effort into planning and planting the perfect flower garden, you don't want weeds popping up to spoil the effect. Eliminating weeds before you plant is a key part of preventing later problems.

Weeds in Your Flowers

All gardeners start their flower gardens with great dreams of lush, colorful, fragrant blooms. That's why it's so sad to see spindly flowers surrounded by healthy thistles or invading grass. But you can prepare and care for your beds of annual and perennial flowers in ways that discourage weeds. Then it won't be a big effort to get rid of the few weeds that do manage to grow.

Getting a Good Start

The first steps toward a weed-free flower garden come when you prepare and plant the bed. Careful soil preparation and planting are especially important for perennial gardens since you don't get the chance to start fresh each year as you do with beds of annual flowers.

One key to weed control is remembering that many weed seeds lie buried in your soil. The less you stir up the soil, the fewer new weeds you'll bring to the surface to grow. For perennial beds, you'll really only dig the soil once, so this isn't as much of a concern. But in annual beds, cutting down on digging can dramatically reduce your weed problems.

As you work with your soil, you'll get a feel for how often it needs to be turned. If the soil is heavy and high in clay, try turning it once a year to a depth of about 8 inches (20 cm), adding organic

Weeds can hide the beauty of your flowers.

matter such as weed-seed-free compost to loosen the soil. If your soil is crumbly and loose or high in sand, try turning it every other year. During the year you don't turn it, just dig a hole for individual annuals.

Because the roots of perennial flowers grow deep into the soil, a new perennial bed needs one very thorough digging. Double-digging—turning the soil to the depth of two spade blades (about 16 inches [40 cm] deep)—is usually recommended for perennial beds. As long as you're that deep into the soil, take the opportunity to remove root parts belonging to perennial weeds.

Keeping ahead of the Weeds

The best way to deal with weeds is to not have to deal with them at all. By mulching, you can keep most weeds in check. And by installing an edging strip, you'll keep your lawn grass from becoming a weed among your flowers.

Managing Mulches Effectively Some mulches are better than others for flower beds. The best do more

---

A Shady Trick

It can take a few years for newly planted perennials to fill in their bed. To keep weeds from invading the bare spaces, transplant annuals between the new perennials. The fast-growing annuals will shade the soil so weed seeds don't get enough light to sprout.

Avoid leaving bare soil; mulch or plant empty spots.

As you dig, pull out any weed roots you find in the soil.

If weeds get out of hand, dig up your plants and start over.

Stones and gravel make attractive mulches for rock gardens.

Low, bushy perennials such as catmints (*Nepeta* spp.) are great as weed-suppressing groundcovers under roses, shrubs, and trees.

than just protect the soil—they also make an attractive background for your plants. (And what's the point of planting pretty flowers if you're going to surround them with an ugly mulch?) Hold off applying mulches until the stems are sturdy—usually in mid- to late-spring. Then keep mulching materials 1 to 2 inches (2.5 to 5 cm) away from flower stems to avoid stem rot.

Some of the best mulches for flower gardens are discussed below. For more mulching tips, see "The Mulch Miracle" on page 36.

- **Bark** looks good and lasts a long time. Bark nuggets are the best for weed control and are less likely than shredded bark or bark chips to splash onto pavement when it rains.

- **Cocoa bean shells** have a nice dark color and are easy to handle. Some people don't like the odor of the fresh shells; others enjoy the chocolate aroma; either way, you'll usually only smell it for a few days. The fresh shells can blow around if you use them in a windy spot. They break down quickly, so you may need to add another layer in mid- to late-summer.

- **Leaves** look right at home nestled around perennials. Shredded leaves break down faster than whole ones and are less likely to become matted and slimy, but you need a thicker layer to suppress weeds.

- **Pecan shells** last a long time and are heavy enough to stay put when the wind blows. On the down side, they sometimes attract squirrels, which may dig up plants.

- **Pine needles** are pretty, especially around perennials, but you need to spread them about 6 inches (15 cm) deep to keep weeds down. Don't collect needles from

Avoid piling mulch right around plant stems.

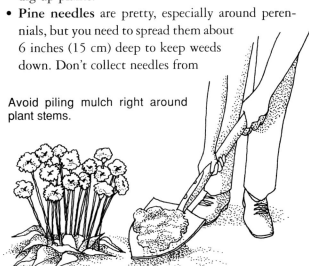

Wipe Out Weeds before You Dig

If you plan to locate your flower bed where a nasty stand of perennial weeds once stood, you'll save yourself future grief if you take the time to grow a smother crop for a season or solarize the soil before you plant. For details on these methods, see "Choke Out Weeds with Smother Crops" on page 32 and "Bake Away Your Weeds" on page 30.

pine forests; get them from a reputable source or gather them from under your own trees.

If you have aggressive perennial weeds, such as thistles (*Cirsium* spp.) or johnson grass (*Sorghum halepense*), in an established bed, you have a few options. The most effective but least practical option is to dig up all of the plants, solarize or grow a smother crop, and then replant. A more practical approach is to break out the heavy-duty mulches to smother them. Cut the weeds to the ground, and remove as much of the root system as you can without digging up your good plants. Cover the weeded area with newspaper or black plastic, then top that with whatever mulch you're using in the rest of the bed.

Excluding Weeds with Edgings To keep your lawn from creeping into the flower bed, install edging strips. If you grow a well-behaved cool-season

Loosestrifes *(Lythrum* spp.) have showy magenta flowers, but they can be serious weeds; avoid planting them.

grass, such as perennial ryegrass or bluegrass, a border of bricks or landscape timbers will suffice. Set the edging so its top is just slightly above the soil surface. When you mow, run the wheels on one side of the mower along the strip to trim the edge.

If you live in the South, where most grasses are aggressive spreaders, the edging strip needs to extend 3 inches (7.5 cm) below the soil and 3 inches (7.5 cm) above. You can use large stone blocks or the flat plastic or metal strips that are sold at garden centers. Use hand trimmers or an edging tool to trim grass runners that try to creep over the strip.

Hands-on Control

There comes a time when, despite your best efforts at prevention, a weed will have the audacity to appear among your flowers. The best time to control these uninvited guests is when

---

A Fishy End to Water-garden Weeds

Aquatic weeds growing in ponds present a real challenge: What do you do, hoe while you row? For many weeds, fish are the answer.

The mud carp (*Cyprinus carpio*), a scavenger that feeds along the muddy bottoms of ponds and lakes, uproots submersed aquatic weeds as it forages. It can also break up algae mats.

The white amur (*Ctenopharyngodon idella*) is one of the few herbivorous fish that can tolerate winter temperatures and water of poor quality. It feeds on a variety of aquatic weeds.

In freshwater that doesn't get below 50°F (10°C), a large snail (*Marisa cornuarietis*) cleans up many weeds, including common coontail (*Ceratophyllum demersum*), Illinois pondweed (*Potamogeton illinoensis*), southern naiad (*Najas guadalupensis*), and salvinia (*Salvinia rotundifolia*).

If you're interested in adding fish or snails to your water feature, you can find more information in books on water gardening. Local or mail-order businesses that sell water-gardening supplies may also be able to recommend the right choices for your particular conditions.

Controlling weeds early in the season will give your flowers a chance to fill in and grow strongly.

If you don't catch weeds when they're small, they can quickly take over, giving your garden a messy look.

Keep perennials healthy and vigorous by spreading a layer of compost over the bed before mulching.

they're small. Early control is particularly beneficial with perennial weeds. As perennial weed seedlings mature, they begin to store energy in their roots; this stored energy enables established perennials to keep resprouting even after repeated cutting. You have a variety of control options to choose from for handling these vegetative invaders, including hand-pulling, hoeing, and flaming. For details on these and other hands-on weed control techniques, see "Take a Physical Approach" on page 26.

Some flowers can reseed prolifically. Pull out unwanted seedlings or move them to other parts of the garden.

Fertilizing Mulched Flowers

Many of the mulches that suppress weeds and look attractive—including bark and pecan shells—don't release nutrients fast enough to do your plants much good. That's because these long-lasting materials are low in nitrogen, one of the nutrients plants need. Take one of these approaches to make sure your mulched flowers are also well fed:

- Work fertilizer into the soil at planting time. For annuals, use a material that releases nutrients fairly quickly, such as a commercially available organic fertilizer. For perennials and bulbs, use slow-release materials such as compost, aged manure, bonemeal, and granite meal.
- If you didn't fertilize your annuals at planting time or if your established perennials and bulbs need a boost, spread fertilizer or compost on the soil surface before covering the soil with mulch.
- During the growing season, give weak or slow-growing plants a shot of liquid fertilizer. Pour diluted fish emulsion on the soil or spray it on the leaves. Liquid fertilizers can supplement dry ones applied to the soil; as a supplement, apply them once or twice during the season. If you use liquid fertilizers exclusively (not the best option), apply them every 3 to 4 weeks.

Feverfew (*Chrysanthemum parthenium*) is loved for its masses of white flowers but not for its rampant reseeding.

The dainty pink blooms of herb Robert (*Geranium robertianum*) mature into seeds that spread far and wide.

When Good Plants Turn Bad

As gardeners, it's satisfying to watch our young plants thrive and expand to fill in the empty spaces around them. It's also rewarding to get a lot of plants for a little money. That's why many of us like flowers and groundcovers that spread quickly and cover as much ground as two or three slower plants would.

The disadvantage of these fast-spreading plants is that they sometimes cross the line between vigorous and aggressive. These spreaders eventually begin invading areas where we never meant for them to be.

From Treasures to Thugs

The best way to avoid problems is to only plant fast-creeping, invasive plants where they have enough room to spread out. That way, their natural tendencies work for your landscape, not against it.

This approach doesn't always work, however. You may have grown a plant in a previous garden where it behaved itself, only to discover that the growing conditions at your new house are so much more favorable that the thing has crawled over the fence and halfway down the street before you've shaken the soil from the spade.

The other problem is that some aggressive plants are so *cute* that you can't help but plant them in some tiny corner right near the front door. After all, who can resist the dainty blooms of violets, the quaint,

---

From Flower Seed to Weed

Some flowers—including spider flower (*Cleome hassleriana*), forget-me-nots (*Myosotis* spp.), and morning glories (*Ipomoea* spp.)—reseed so prolifically that they can become weeds. A coarse mulch should stop most of the weeds from reaching the soil. But if you want to be certain those seeds don't even get a chance to drop, remove the flowers once they turn brown or pinch off the developing seedpods. This practice, called deadheading, can also help your plants bloom longer.

Lily-of-the-valley (*Convallaria majalis*) is a great groundcover in large areas but can become invasive.

Bee balm (*Monarda didyma*) thrives in moist soil; divide it every year or two to keep it under control.

old-fashioned fragrance of lily-of-the-valley, or the soft, fuzzy leaves of lamb's-ears? Unfortunately, what seemed like a charming idea at planting time quickly becomes a real maintenance headache.

Taking Control

If you know what makes a plant invasive, you can take steps to keep it under control. A few potentially weedy ornamentals—such as feverfew (*Chrysanthemum parthenium*) and herb Robert (*Geranium robertianum*)—invade by producing lots of seed and lots of seedlings. Others have runners, either aboveground (called stolons) or underground (called rhizomes), that enable the parent plant to send up new plants without going to the trouble of flowering and setting seed. Bee balm (*Monarda didyma*), ajugas (*Ajuga* spp.), and goutweed (*Aegopodium podagraria*) are a few garden plants that spread by runners.

To control plants that spread by producing a lot of seed, you need to keep the seed from reaching the soil. A bark nugget mulch is usually sufficient; for added protection, spread plastic sheeting or a few layers of newspaper on the ground before putting down the mulch.

When you plant an aggressive perennial flower or ground-cover that has runners, put it by itself in a bed, then surround the bed with an edging strip that extends a few inches above and below the ground. Or create a broad barrier with tightly spaced bricks set so that the long sides are side by side. You can combine edging strips

> ## The Invaders
> A surprising number of common garden plants can become real weed problems in certain conditions. If you want to grow these aggressive spreaders, plant them where they have plenty of room, contain them, or cut them back often so they don't creep or seed out of bounds.
>
> Listed below are a few garden plants that can cover large areas surprisingly quickly. You may want to check with other gardeners or with your local Cooperative Extension Service to find out which of these and other plants can become serious problems in your area.
>
> *Achillea millefolium* (yarrow)
> *Aegopodium podagraria* (goutweed)
> *Ajuga reptans* (ajuga)
> Bamboos
> *Chasmanthium latifolium* (northern sea oats)
> *Chrysanthemum parthenium* (feverfew)
> *Convallaria majalis* (lily-of-the-valley)
> *Coronilla varia* (crown vetch)
> *Cortaderia jubata* (purple pampas grass)
> *Dennstaedtia punctilobula* (hay-scented fern)
> *Hedera helix* (English ivy)
> *Lysimachia clethroides* (gooseneck loosestrife)
> *Macleaya* spp. (plume poppies)
> *Mentha* spp. (mints)
> *Nepeta cataria* (catnip)
> *Oenothera speciosa* (showy evening primrose)
> *Onoclea sensibilis* (sensitive fern)
> *Ornithogalum umbellatum* (star-of-Bethlehem)
> *Pennisetum alopecuroides* (fountain grass)
> *Phalaris arundinacea* 'Picta' (ribbon grass)
> *Ranunculus ficaria* (lesser celandine)
> *Stachys byzantina* (lamb's-ears)
> *Stylophorum diphyllum* (wood poppy)
> *Viola* spp. (violets)

and brick strips for double security. An alternative for plants that spread under the surface is to grow them in bottomless pots or buckets sunk into the soil.

If you are willing to go to the bother, frequent division can keep spreading plants in bounds. Every few years, dig out the plants, divide them, and replant some of the divisions into the prepared site. Plant the remaining divisions elsewhere, compost them, or give them to someone who can use them.

Stopping Weeds under Trees and Shrubs

Controlling weeds around trees and shrubs generally isn't a major landscape problem, since the ground around the base of these plants is often dry and shady. You may choose a decorative mulch, a weed barrier, or a groundcover to discourage weeds from sprouting. Occasional hand-pulling is all you'll need to control any weeds that do pop up through the mulch or groundcover.

Apply a Mulch

A coarse-textured mulch under trees and shrubs is enough to suppress most weeds. Choose a mulch that is attractive enough to fit into your landscape. Bark nuggets look good and are one of the most effective

Heart-leaved bergenia (*Bergenia cordifolia*) makes an excellent groundcover under trees and shrubs.

mulches for stopping weeds. A 3- to 4-inch layer (7.5 to 10 cm) of mulch is ideal. If you use less, it won't be as effective at controlling weeds; if you use more, you can smother the tree or shrub roots. For more details on choosing, applying, and maintaining mulches, see "The Mulch Miracle" on page 36.

Lay a Weed Barrier

An alternative to a thick layer of mulch is to use a dense barrier such as newspaper or landscape fabric. You can either put the barrier down when you plant or install it later. Cover the barrier with a thin layer of a decorative mulch, such as bark or stones.

Leave a mulch-free zone at the base of the trunk to prevent rot.

Stopping Tree Seedlings

Some trees produce seeds that pop up all over the yard, especially in ornamental beds and lawn areas. A few of the weedy-seed trees are maples (especially Norway maple [*Acer platanoides*] and silver maple [*A. saccharinum*]), some birches (*Betula* spp.), poplars (*Populus* spp.), black alder (*Alnus glutinosa*), tree-of-heaven (*Ailanthus altissima*), and black locust (*Robinia pseudoacacia*). Here are some solutions:

- Mow regularly. Mowing usually takes care of tree seedlings in the lawn. They may survive a few cuttings, but eventually they give up.

- Grow a lawn grass that produces natural toxins that inhibit tree seedlings; these allelopathic grasses include tall fescue (*Festuca arundinacea*), annual ryegrass (*Lolium multiflorum*), and perennial ryegrass (*Lolium perenne*).

- In ornamental beds, a 4-inch (10 cm) mulch of bark nuggets should keep most tree seeds from reaching the soil.

- Instead of flower beds, plant a dense groundcover or close-growing, low shrubs under weedy trees to shade out the seeds.

- When possible, avoid future problems by planting seedless tree cultivars.

Trees and shrubs make their own mulch. Rake up leaves in fall and chop them for use as weed-suppressing mulch.

Mowing regularly can control tree seedlings in lawn areas.

Sun-loving lawn grasses tend to grow weakly under trees, leaving space for weeds to grow; replace them with more vigorous shade-loving plants.

Barriers block organic matter from returning to the soil to feed plants, so consider spreading a layer of compost over the soil before applying the barrier. Use a liquid fertilizer like fish emulsion to feed mulched trees and shrubs.

Grow a Groundcover

If you want something alive under your trees and shrubs, grow a groundcover that forms a thick cover over the ground, shading out weeds. Or let your lawn grow close to your trees. Just keep the grass a foot or two (30 to 60 cm) away from the base of the plant so you don't nick the trunk when you mow. Use mulch or a weed barrier to cover the soil between the lawn and the trunk.

If All Else Fails

To kill weeds that make it through the mulch or groundcover, hand-pulling works well. Flaming can work if the leaves of the tree or shrub won't get in your way; they can be damaged by the heat, too. Don't use boiling water, vinegar, or salt to kill weeds under trees; all three can do serious damage to delicate feeder roots that grow near the surface.

Use plants or mulch to keep weeds from growing around the base of trees and shrubs.

Mix hardy cyclamen (*Cyclamen repandum*) with wildflowers under trees to crowd out weeds.

Coping with Woody Weeds

What is it that makes one tree, shrub, or vine a desirable landscape plant and another a weed? It may be the way a tree grows, the habits it has, or the pests it attracts.

Some woody plants spread far and fast, climbing over or crowding out mild-mannered plants in their path. (For more on these pushy plants, see "Weedy Woody Plants.") Others are messy. They may drop parts of themselves, such as twigs, flowers, seedpods, and seeds. Mimosa (*Albizia julibrissin*), for instance, is a pretty tree, but it spends half of the year dropping spent flowers and pods onto the ground below. Silver maple (*Acer saccharinum*) has brittle branches that scatter twigs after every windy storm. And female ginkgos (*Ginkgo biloba*) drop a putrid-smelling fruit.

Some trees and shrubs are a bother because they attract hordes of insects. Among the best known in this category are some willows, with the tiny, round, metallic blue elm beetle, and box elder (*Acer negundo*), with its dark, red-marked box elder bugs that cling to the sides of houses when not in the tree.

Choose a Control

Weedy vines, trees, and shrubs are tough to control because they defy most of the weed control techniques

Mimosa (*Albizia julibrissin*) is attractive in bloom, but it drops a lot of debris and reseeds readily.

that lay waste to soft-stemmed, herbaceous weeds. Their stems are too tough to pull, hoe, or flame except when the plant is a young seedling.

If you're just trying to keep the plant under control, cut unwanted shoots to the ground regularly and ruthlessly. This can work on many shrubs and vines, including wisteria (*Wisteria* spp.), trumpet vine (*Campsis radicans*), and amur honeysuckle (*Lonicera maackii*).

In some cases, removing the problem plant may be the best option. For many trees, shrubs, and vines, cutting them down and removing the stump is all it takes. Digging out the stump is a lot of work, but then you

Cut back unwanted wisteria shoots at ground level.

won't have to worry about new shoots sprouting from it. Shrubs and vines are easier than trees—all you need is a sturdy pick and some upper-body strength. To remove large tree stumps, you may need to rent a stump-grinding machine.

The greatest challenge comes when you want to completely get rid of shrubs and vines that spread by underground stems, such as sumacs (*Rhus* spp.) and wisteria. When you see little sumacs and wisterias sprouting up, dig up their roots, tracing them back to where the parent plant was. Or try dousing the area

Staghorn sumac (*Rhus typhina*) looks fine in natural areas, but its suckering habit is a problem in small yards.

Some maples are attractive garden plants; others are weak-wooded and produce many unwanted seedlings.

with boiling water, if you don't mind killing other plants that are living near the sucker shoots.

Live with Woody Weeds

In some cases, you might prefer to live with a weedy tree or shrub rather than get rid of it, especially if it provides shade or the yard would be bare without it.

"Living with" doesn't have to mean "suffering with"; you can do things to make the plant more tolerable. On weak-wooded trees that drop branches and twigs—such as silver maples—prune the tree so the strongest branches remain. If messy fruit is the problem, consider planting a groundcover beneath the tree to conceal the litter.

At times, you might deliberately plant a weedy tree because it serves a short-term purpose. A row of Lombardy poplar (*Populus nigra* 'Italica')—a short-lived, weak-wooded tree— makes a fast-growing temporary screen or windbreak. When you set out the poplars, plant another row of slower-growing, more desirable trees nearby; when the good trees are big enough, cut down the poplars.

Vigorous wisteria can smother trees.

Weedy Woody Plants

Any tree, shrub, or vine growing where you don't want it can be called a weed. But the plants on this list have traits that are particularly undesirable: They may have messy fruit, seeds, or flowers, or they may spread too quickly. Some wrap around trees, hugging them so tightly that water can't move properly from the tree roots to the leaves.

Japanese honeysuckle (*Lonicera japonica*) grows rapidly and can smother shrubs and small trees. To control it, cut the vines back to the ground, then dig out as much of the crown and roots as you can. Cut back any new sprouts every 2 weeks until they stop resprouting.

Norway maple (*Acer platanoides*) is widely planted for quick shade, but it can create real problems. This tree casts dense shade and has wide-spreading, shallow roots, so it's very difficult to grow plants beneath it. It also self-sows prolifically. If you can, cut down the tree; remove the stump or cut down new sprouts every 2 weeks.

Sumacs—especially staghorn (*Rhus typhina*) and smooth (*R. glabra*)—are quick-growing, tall shrubs that spread by suckers and seed. They have an attractive shape, leaf, and fruit, but they can quickly form a tangled thicket if not contained. Cutting unwanted shoots to the ground often produces denser growth the following year. To really get rid of the plants, you need to dig up the roots.

Tree-of-heaven (*Ailanthus altissima*) reseeds heavily and grows into a thicket that can crowd out other trees. Cut down the saplings while the bark is still soft. Cut down any new shoots every 2 weeks until no more sprouts appear.

Wisteria (*Wisteria* spp.) twines aggressively, wrapping around and choking nearby trees if not cut back once or twice a year. It also produces many seeds and has runners that spread along or just below the soil, sending up new plants. If you must grow wisteria, be on the lookout for suckers and seedlings, and pull or dig them out as soon as you spot them.

WEEDS IN LAWNS AND GROUNDCOVERS

Considering all the advertising money spent on promoting weed killers for lawns, you might think that lawn weeds are a major threat to the health and beauty of your landscape. In truth, though, established lawns are one of the easiest places to keep weeds under control. The secret is to keep your lawn healthy and vigorous, so the grass is thick enough that few weeds can squeeze through.

How you care for your lawn week by week decides how healthy and weed-free it will be. The way you mow, water, and fertilize makes the difference between a weak, weed-plagued lawn and one that you're happy living with. Developing a healthy lawn does *not* mean that you have to spend a lot of time on it. In fact, the fussing that many people direct at their lawns—in the form of frequent sprinkling and heavy fertilizing—can actually encourage diseases and insects, which weaken the lawn and make room for weeds.

A healthy lawn requires a reasonable approach to care that takes into account how grass grows. It's important to remember that grasses are unique, tough plants that evolved where they routinely endured heat, drought, grazing, and fires. Grasses can survive heat and drought by going dormant—they stop growing and often turn brown, living in a sort of suspended animation until conditions improve. They tolerate mowing, which is the modern equivalent of grazing and fire, because their growing point is just below the soil, not at the tip of the stem as it is on many plants. By understanding how your lawn grasses naturally respond to stress and by using the techniques explained in "Preventing Lawn Weeds" on page 66, you'll be able to make smart lawn-care decisions and discourage weed problems.

Preventing weeds from getting started is one important step in having a great-looking lawn. But unless you're lucky enough to already have a perfect lawn, you probably have some weeds that you'd like to get rid of. In "Controlling Lawn Weeds" on page 70, you'll also learn what techniques work for getting rid of existing lawn weeds right away while you're waiting for your lawn to become healthy enough to smother them.

One sneaky way to avoid problems with lawn weeds is to eliminate your lawn—or at least part of it. Cutting back on your total lawn area—and replacing the unneeded lawn with easy-care groundcovers—can give you more time for maintaining and enjoying the remaining turf. Groundcovers don't require regular mowing, and many thrive in shady conditions that turf grasses struggle in. Well-chosen, established groundcovers are quite weed-resistant, although they are generally not completely weed-proof. In "Weeds in Groundcovers" on page 71, you'll find tips for controlling weeds in new and established groundcover plantings.

Some people prefer a perfect-looking lawn; others don't mind a more casual mixture of grasses and flowers. Decide what kind of lawn you can live with and plan your weed control strategies accordingly.

Preventing Lawn Weeds

As in other areas of your yard, controlling weeds in your lawn starts with prevention. If you use the techniques for proper mowing, watering, and fertilizing explained here, your lawn will naturally be more vigorous and will shade out most weeds before they even get a chance to sprout.

Mowing

Not many plants are adapted to survive regular mowing. Grasses can take it because their growing point is just below the soil rather than at the tip of the stem. Although grasses tolerate being cut, mowing does cause some stress because it removes a portion of the leaf blade—the part of the plant that collects sunlight and produces food for new growth.

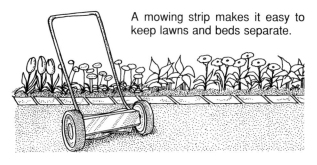

A mowing strip makes it easy to keep lawns and beds separate.

To keep your lawn healthy, remember two rules— mow high, and mow only when you have to. Not only will you leave enough leaf blade to collect light and make food but you'll also enable the lawn to shade its roots from the summer sun. Different grasses thrive at

If a weed-free lawn is important to you, you'll need to invest more time in scouting for and controlling seedling weeds.

different heights; for recommended mowing heights, see "Hit the Right Height." You can cut actively growing grasses a little shorter than those that are nearly dormant.

To reduce stress on grasses, mow your lawn only when it really needs to be trimmed. The rule of thumb is to mow when the grass is one-third taller than the recommended mowing height. So, if the mowing height for your lawn is 2 inches (5 cm) tall, mow when the grass is 3 inches (7.5 cm) tall. By removing only one-third of the blade, you minimize how often the grass has to recover from a mowing while leaving enough leaf blade to produce food for healthy, vigorous growth.

Mowing your lawn regularly at the right height will keep it vigorous and naturally less susceptible to weed problems.

Buttercups (*Ranunculus* spp.) are common weeds in wet spots, where lawn grasses tend to grow poorly.

If you don't enjoy English daisies (*Bellis perennis*) in your lawn, dig out the rosettes as soon as you see them.

Watering

Water usually isn't lacking in the spring and fall, when rain keeps the grass green. The question of how to water comes up during the heat and dryness of summer. And the answer depends on whether you want the lawn to stay green or don't mind a dormant, healthy but possibly browned lawn.

To keep the lawn green, water deeply when dry areas of the yard look dull and the grass doesn't spring back right away when you step on it. Water until the soil is wet about 6 inches (15 cm) down. To test, poke a skewer or screwdriver into the soil; if it penetrates easily to 5 or 6 inches (12.5 to 15 cm) or hits rock (for gardeners in the West or Southwest), the water has gone deep enough.

To simply keep the roots and crowns of dormant lawns alive *without* greening them up, apply ½ inch (1.25 cm) of water every 6 to 8 weeks if temperatures are moderate. During hot weather, apply the same amount every 3 weeks.

Either watering strategy ensures that the sod will be vigorous enough to block weeds when it really matters—in spring, early summer, and fall.

Use a metal probe to check soil moisture.

Whichever approach you choose, the water may begin running off onto the pavement before it can soak deep enough, especially if you have tight, clayey soil. If you see any runoff, turn off the water for about 1 hour, then resume watering.

Hit the Right Height

Mowing height is the distance between the cutting blade and the soil. To check the height of your mower blade, set the mower on a flat surface, such as a driveway, and slip a board of known height under the mower to check the clearance.

This list includes mowing heights based on periods of active and slow growth. In the North, where cool-season grasses are commonly grown, the active period is in the spring and fall; during the heat of summer, grass grows slowly. Southern warm-season grasses are most active during late spring, summer (if they get enough water), and early fall; they go dormant once the weather cools and during the heat of summer if they don't get water.

Northern Grasses
- Bent grass: ¾ inch (2 cm) when active; 1 inch (2.5 cm) when slow
- Kentucky bluegrass: 2 inches (5 cm) when active; 2½ to 3 inches (6.25 to 7.5 cm) when slow
- Perennial ryegrass: 2 inches (5 cm) when active; 2½ to 3 inches (6.25 to 7.5 cm) when slow
- Red fescue: 2 inches (5 cm) when active; 2½ inches (6.25 cm) when slow
- Tall fescue: 2½ inches (6.25 cm) when active; 3 inches (7.5 cm) when slow

Southern Grasses
- Bermuda grass: ¾ to 1 inch (2 to 2.5 cm) when active; 1½ inches (3.75 cm) when slow
- Centipede grass: 1½ inches (3.75 cm) when active; 2 inches (5 cm) when slow
- St. Augustine grass: 2 inches (5 cm) when active; 3 inches (7.5 cm) when slow
- Zoysia: 1 inch (2.5 cm) when active; 1½ inches (3.75 cm) when slow

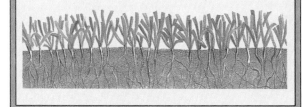

Starting a Weed-free Lawn

If you're starting a new lawn, you have two main options: seed or sod. Laying sod (pieces of already-growing grass) is fast and provides an immediate dense soil cover, but it is expensive. If your budget is limited, you can start a new lawn inexpensively by spreading seed over bare soil. With some Southern grasses, you can also plant sprigs or plugs of grass, a technique that's halfway between seeding and sodding. Any way you go, preparing the site correctly and planting properly will get your lawn off to the most vigorous start possible.

1. Dig out all visible weeds, including all the roots you can see.

2. Level the site, moving soil from high spots to low spots with a rake or shovel.

3. Rake the soil smooth with a metal rake.

4. Water the area, then wait 7 to 10 days for weed seeds near the surface to sprout. Hoe those weeds. Repeat the watering, waiting, and hoeing routine once or twice more.

5. Spread the seed, plant the sprigs or plugs, or lay the sod. If you're seeding the lawn, broadcast the seed at the recommended rate, spreading half in one direction and the other half perpendicular to the first direction.

6. If you planted seed or used sod, go over the area with a roller to make good contact between the new planting and the soil.

7. Mulch newly seeded, sprigged, or plugged areas to conserve moisture and keep soil from washing away. Straw is the traditional mulch. You can also use a polyester blanket, like the spun-bonded row covers commonly seen in vegetable gardens.

8. Water immediately and water often while the grass becomes established. For seeded lawns, sprinkle the area lightly a few times a day to keep the soil moist until the seedlings get established. For sod, sprigs, or plugs, water twice a week. After 4 weeks, you can water less often—every week or two. After the first few mowings, the lawn should be established; then water only as needed during dry spells.

Fertilizing

The grasses that grew wild on the prairie were fertilized by the decaying leaf blades and stems of previous years' growth. You can fertilize your lawn in a similar fashion by letting the grass clippings fall back onto the lawn. If you don't want to invest in a mulching mower, see if your mower can be fitted with a mulching blade—most mowers made since the late 1980s can be. If you don't leave the grass clippings on your lawn or if your grass is pale and weak-looking, supplement it with an organic fertilizer. You can spread well-decomposed compost or composted manure over the lawn after rubbing it through a screen to break up the big chunks. Or you can spread a commercial organic lawn fertilizer, which is less bulky than compost or manure. If your lawn is particularly weedy and unhealthy, try an organic fertilizer that contains encapsulated microorganisms, such as Ringer's Lawn Restore. It gives a boost to the population of soil microorganisms, which break down decaying plant material into the nutrients living plants need.

How much fertilizer you have to apply depends on many different factors, including your soil type, the kind of grass you grow, and how much it rains. As a starting point, apply 2 pounds (4.5 kg) of actual nitrogen per 1,000 square feet (93 sq m) of lawn each year. Decrease the amount next year if that rate makes the lawn a deep blue-green color. If the

Laying sod is a fast way to establish a new lawn. Weeds never get a chance to sprout before the soil is covered.

Field chickweed (*Cerastium arvense*) is a troublesome weed in grassy areas. Dig it out before it sets seed.

lawn is a normal green, the rate is about right.

When you are working with organic lawn fertilizers, you don't have to be especially exact; you can usually get good results from estimating how much to apply. But if you like to be precise, you can figure out how much to apply with a few calculations.

To calculate actual nitrogen in a bag of fertilizer, multiply the total weight of the bag by the percentage of nitrogen in the fertilizer (the first of the three numbers on the label). Then multiply the weight of the bag by 2 and divide by the pounds of actual nitrogen to see how many pounds of fertilizer to apply per 1,000 square feet (93 sq m).

For example, a 50-pound (25 kg) bag of 7-4-3 fertilizer would contain 3½ pounds (1.5 kg) of actual nitrogen (50 x 0.07 = 3.5). Multiply 50 pounds by 2 (because you need 2 pounds), divide by 3.5, and you'll find that you need to apply about 30 pounds (15 kg) of fertilizer per 1,000 square feet (93 sq m).

If you fertilize once a year, you can apply the material in spring or fall. An alternative is to split the annual application, applying half in spring and half in fall. The split application is extra work, but it ensures a more even supply of nutrients to your lawn.

Temporary Green for Southern Lawns
The warm-season grasses grown in the South don't turn green until late spring, long after the early weeds have gotten a good head start. To keep ahead of the weeds, sow seed of cool-season annual rye (*Lolium multiflorum*) over the lawn in late fall or early spring. It grows early enough to compete with weeds, then dies when the hot weather hits and the warm-season grasses start growing.

Common chickweed (*Stellaria media*) is a lawn invader that thrives in the cool temperatures of spring and fall.

Controlling Lawn Weeds

While you're waiting for your new lawn-care program to choke out weeds or if you want to get rid of the few weeds that make it past even the healthiest lawn, you can use more direct methods.

Several of the techniques covered in detail in "Weed Control Options," starting on page 22, are effective against lawn weeds; these include hand-pulling, digging, flaming, organic herbicides, boiling water, and—in extreme cases—solarization. If your method leaves any bare spots bigger than a few inches across, scatter grass seed over them and keep the seed moist for about 3 weeks. Or dig patches of sod from healthy but out-of-sight parts of the lawn to cover the spots before weeds have a chance to return.

A combination of good gardening techniques and organic weed control methods will give you a lawn that's attractive and chemical-free.

Hand-pulling and Digging

Pulling works pretty well for controlling most weeds. Even if you only get the aboveground parts, you'll weaken the weed because it has to spend energy to regrow. If the soil is moist and you're lucky enough to get the whole root, all the better.

For perennial weeds, digging is more effective. For taprooted weeds like dandelion, use a dandelion weeder to pop the taproot out of moist soil. To get rid of weeds with creeping roots, like red sorrel (*Rumex acetosella*), try digging them up, being sure to get as much of the underground portion as possible.

"Pulling and Digging" on page 26 offers more tips on these techniques.

Flaming

Grasses tolerate heat better than other plants, so if you briefly flame a broad-leaved seedling, the surrounding lawn should recover. For details on this technique, see "Fighting Weeds with Fire" on page 29.

Using Natural Herbicides and Boiling Water

Organic herbicides are most effective on annual seedlings; if spray gets on the adjacent lawn, established grass will turn brown for a while but won't die. You could use cardboard or plastic to protect the lawn while you spray nearby young annuals; however, it's usually easier to just pull out the weeds than to go to that bother.

Boiling water kills everything it touches, so reserve it for small, hopeless patches of really bad weeds, then reseed or resod.

One exciting product is a natural herbicide for controlling lawn weeds. This material is actually corn gluten meal, a by-product of the grain milling process. It acts as a pre-emergent herbicide, which means that it kills developing weed seedlings before they get established; it does not control established weeds. Corn gluten meal is harmless to people and pets. Plus, it adds nitrogen to your lawn as it breaks down.

This material is sold under the name A-Maizing Lawn. Apply it in spring and fall, according to package directions. Or, if you have access to corn gluten meal through a local feed mill, you could try applying it at 20 pounds per 1,000 square feet (10 kg per 93 sq m).

Solarizing the Soil

Solarization, which is described in "Bake Away Your Weeds" on page 30, heats up the top layer of soil, killing many weed seeds and roots as well as good and bad soil organisms. Reserve this technique for large, hopeless patches of really bad weeds. Replant the area, as explained in "Starting a Weed-free Lawn" on page 68.

Weeds in Groundcovers

Groundcovers can be great low-maintenance plants for your landscape. Grow them under trees and shrubs to cover the soil and discourage weeds. Use them as barriers between lawns and garden areas to keep grass out of flower or vegetable beds. Let them spread over slopes and other tough sites where less vigorous garden plants won't grow. When you choose groundcovers that are adapted to the site and the growing conditions you have to offer, they can form dense mats of foliage that shade the soil and discourage weed development.

But even though most established groundcovers are weed-resistant, they aren't always completely weed-proof. And new groundcover plantings can be prone to weeds until they fill in to cover the bare soil. A combination of prevention and control will help to keep all of your groundcovers looking their best.

Preventing Weed Problems

When you prepare an area for a groundcover planting, get rid of as many weeds as possible before you start. On flat land, you can use the weed seed–sprouting method described in Step 4 of "Starting a Weed-free Lawn" on page 68. On sloping land, which is more prone to erosion, it's risky to leave the soil bare long enough to let weeds sprout. You could try covering the slope with a layer of clear plastic for a few weeks; the extra heat will encourage weed seeds to sprout and then kill the tender seedlings. Remove the plastic and set out your plants.

Some groundcovers—like low-growing junipers

In the right growing conditions, creeping thyme (*Thymus* spp.) can form an attractive and effective groundcover.

(*Juniper* spp.)—grow from a central stem with branches that spread out over the ground. For these, you can use a dense mulch, such as landscape fabric, that forms a relatively permanent barrier on top of the soil. Lay the barrier over the unplanted bed and cut a hole for each plant. Cover the barrier with a more decorative mulch until the plants fill in.

Most groundcovers spread outward from the parent plants, either by creeping roots or rooting stems. Barrier mulches don't work for these kinds of plantings since they'll discourage your groundcover as well as the weeds. Instead, use a thin mulch that breaks down fairly quickly, such as straw or pine needles. It also helps to set the plants out at the closest recommended spacings. Most groundcovers take 2 or 3 years to fill in; while you wait, plant flowering annuals in the empty spaces to shade out weeds.

Controlling Groundcover Weeds

Although groundcovers don't grow as dense as grasses do, they shade out most weeds once established; for weeds that get through, hand-pulling works well. You can use organic herbicides, if you're willing to protect the groundcover from damage with cardboard or plastic.

A yearly sweep through your groundcover plantings should catch most weeds before they get too well established. If a tough perennial weed like Canada thistle (*Cirsium arvense*) does get started, pull or dig out as much as you can; repeat the process every 2 weeks until no more sprouts appear. If the weeds are especially persistent or enmeshed in the planting, the best approach is to dig up the area, solarize it (as explained in "Bake Away Your Weeds" on page 30), and start over.

A layer of landscape fabric can keep weeds from getting established in shrubby groundcover plantings.

Weeds in Fence Lines, Paths, and Paving

When you think about the areas in your yard where weeds are a worry, your vegetable garden might come to mind first, or perhaps your lawn or maybe your flower beds. Probably the last places you think of are the strips of land that border your fences, the pathways that cross your lawn, and those cracks in the sidewalk and driveway.

And while it's true that weeds growing in these low-profile places aren't going to cut your tomato yield in half or choke out the begonias, there are good reasons to keep them in check. Weeds growing in fence lines and pathways provide a source of weed seed that can find its way into other parts of your yard. These areas can also shelter harmful insects and plant diseases. And the weeds growing between cracks in the pavement can contribute to the pavement's deterioration, as well as giving the landscape a scraggly appearance.

But let's face it. Fence lines, paths, and paving are low-priority parts of the yard, and you don't want to spend a lot of time controlling weeds in them. Fortunately, because nothing has to grow in these areas, you can use heavy-duty methods of prevention and control that wouldn't work as well elsewhere.

The idea is to get the weeds under control, then forget about them. If you're really lucky, you'll have the chance to install some long-lasting means of stopping weeds when you put in a new fence, path, or paved area. You'll read about those long-lasting means in "Weeds along Fences" on page 74, "Weeds in Paths and Walkways" on page 76, and "Weeds in Patios and Paving" on page 78.

But most of us inherit our fences and paved areas—and their weed problems—when we buy our house. Or we have a house built but have no say in how fences and pavement are installed. In that case, we must make do after the fact, creating a solution that fits our specific situation. This chapter includes a variety of techniques that you can adapt to your site.

Sometimes we inherit areas that have been neglected rather than ones we want to neglect. You may be confronting an overgrown wooded area, a too-wild meadow, or an old weedy garden. If you are, check out "Weeds in Neglected Areas" on page 80 for ways to tame these wild-and-weedy areas.

It's easy to overlook walls, fences, and paved areas when you're thinking about weed control. But if you want to keep your property looking respectable, it's worth taking a little time to cope with these normally neglected spots.

Weeds along Fences

The problem with controlling weeds along fences is that you can't mow them easily. You could spend a few hours each weekend wrestling with a string trimmer or squeezing grass shears until your hand cramps up. A far better option is to find some way to make the weeds go away on a more permanent basis.

The surest technique is to install a barrier under the fence that weeds can't penetrate. The kind of barrier you use depends on what kind of fence you're building, as well as your own preferences. Although it's easiest to install the barrier when you put up the fence, you can wiggle some barriers into place afterward, if there's enough clearance under the fence.

If you're putting up a wood or wire fence, clear the area below the future fence by hoeing or closely

When not well planned or maintained, fence lines can become an ideal site for weeds to take over.

Barrier Choices

To keep weeds from growing under and beside fences, you can install a weed barrier, then cover it with an attractive mulch.

Black plastic, roofing paper, and landscape fabric are commonly used as barriers. Each has strengths and weaknesses that should be considered before you make your choice.

- **Black plastic** is the least expensive material, but it becomes brittle over time and will rip, leaving spaces for weeds to come up. Black plastic doesn't let water through, so it can cause puddling and get smelly unless you punch small holes in it. Because black plastic is slick, bark mulch can slide off of it on sloping land.
- **Roofing paper** is more durable than black plastic and less expensive than landscape fabric. But it is heavy and difficult to work with, and you need to make the barrier three layers thick.
- **Landscape fabric** comes in different thicknesses so you can choose the best one for each job. It is durable and fairly easy to work with; its higher cost is its biggest drawback.

---

mowing existing weeds. Then lay down a barrier of thick black plastic, landscape fabric, or roofing paper. (See "Barrier Choices" for each material's good and bad points.)

Cover the barrier with gravel, bark chips, or another decorative mulch to anchor and hide it. If your lawn is next to the mulch-covered barrier, choose a mulch material that won't fly too violently if you accidentally get the mower too close to the mulch.

To keep weeds from growing right next to a brick or stone fence, pour a concrete strip beside the base of it. The strip should be wide enough that you can run a wheel of the mower along it without bumping into the fence. If you grow a non-invasive grass, such as most of the Northern lawn grasses, make the concrete strip level with the soil. If you grow an aggressive lawn grass—like bermuda grass or many of the other Southern grasses—raise the concrete strip 2 to 3 inches (5 to 7.5 cm) above the soil level so the grass is less likely to creep over it.

As an alternative to concrete, you can make the mowing strip from bricks or paving stones or spread a layer of gravel

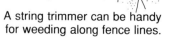

A string trimmer can be handy for weeding along fence lines.

Create a flower bed at the base of a wall or fence to keep weeds away.

Weeds growing in neglected areas along fences are prime sources of weed seed. That seed can spread easily to other parts of your garden.

or bark nuggets over a weed barrier such as landscape fabric. Instead of using a barrier under or along a fence, you could plant a dense, low-growing groundcover, but you'd need to weed it occasionally.

Often you don't have control over what grows on both sides of a fence. If your neighbors grow an aggressive plant that creeps under the fence, install an edging strip that extends a few inches both above and below the soil. If your vegetable garden or ornamental beds abut the fence, mulch those beds well for extra protection. You might even run a band of newspaper, cardboard, black plastic, or landscape fabric along the base of the fence. If appearances matter, hide the barrier with the mulch you use elsewhere in the bed.

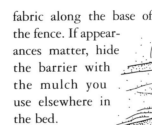

A barrier strip prevents most weeds from creeping under fences.

A well-maintained fence with a barrier strip underneath is an effective divider for different garden areas.

For fence lines, trimming once or twice a year may be the most efficient weed control option.

Weeds in Paths and Walkways

The point of having a pathway is to lead your eye and to guide your feet from one place in the yard to another. That purpose is compromised when a tangle of weeds hides the route. How you cope with a weedy walkway depends on how much foot traffic it gets and what it is made of.

Wood Chips

You can create an attractive, informal path from wood chips in areas that get light to moderate traffic. Wood chip paths are easy to make and relatively inexpensive, especially if you are clearing land and can provide the trees to be chipped. Some fresh chips, especially those from evergreens, may even contain substances that inhibit weeds.

How you prepare the wood chip path depends on the weediness of the area you're covering. If the path will wind through a shady area under trees where little else grows, just pull out or hoe any weeds in the way and dump a 3-inch (7.5 cm) layer of chips on the soil. The chips will smother everything under them. You can use the same method if you're covering a non-aggressive grass, but mow the grass as short as possible first.

A well-maintained, weed-free pathway is pleasant to walk on and adds a welcoming touch to any home.

If you are putting the path through a sunny, weedy area or if you grow a lawn grass that spreads aggressively, you'll need a barrier beneath the chips. Mow the area as short as possible, then put down a layer of thick black plastic or landscape fabric before spreading the wood chips. Because water doesn't pass through black plastic, it can get slimy and smelly under wood chips unless you punch small holes in it. Landscape fabric is porous, but it is more expensive. Depending on the quality of the barrier, it may break down in about 5 years and require replacement.

Lay a barrier before putting down paths to prevent weeds.

To keep the chips from flipping off the path into the grass or adjacent plant beds, install some kind of border along the sides of the path—try railroad ties, planks, stones, or edging strips.

Go over the whole path at least once a year to make sure no weeds are creeping into it from the edges. Hand-pull any weeds that have popped up in the path, and add more wood chips, if needed, to cover the barrier.

Alternatives to wood chips include gravel and crushed seashells. Use them the same way as wood chips.

Bricks, Flagstones, and Pavers

For walkways that get daily traffic, bricks, flagstones, and pavers last longer and are less messy than wood chips.

Low, spreading plants may look nice in paths, but keep in mind that they can creep into your flower beds, too.

If you're installing a new walkway, you can prevent weeds by putting a barrier below it. Use thick black plastic, roofing paper, or a heavy landscape fabric that is designed for use under bricks or pavers. Black plastic is inexpensive, but it grows brittle over time and falls apart. And because it's not porous, you have to punch holes in it so water won't collect in it. Roofing paper lasts longer but is difficult to work with because it's stiff and heavy. Landscape fabric is expensive, but doesn't cause puddling or get slimy and smelly.

If you've inherited a permanent walkway with weeds sprouting up through it, you have a couple of choices. If you want a clean, plant-free look, kill the weeds. Pulling works if the bricks or pavers are widely spaced; it works even better if the soil is moist. Or douse the weeds with boiling water, salt water, or vinegar, as long as the liquid won't drain near the base of your garden plants.

Soap-based organic herbicides are a better option around plants you want to keep; use cardboard or plastic to shield the desirable plants from the spray. For the best results, spray when the weeds are tiny. If you're trying to kill a perennial grass, you'll need to apply it every week or two as the grass starts to green up after the last spraying.

Low-growing plants can soften the edges of paths and steps; just trim them back as needed to keep them under control.

Use boiling water to kill weeds between blocks.

If you want a softer, more natural look to your paved areas, you can plant low-growing flowers, groundcovers, or grasses between the bricks, stones, or pavers. A few plants adapted to this use are creeping thymes, creeping speedwell (*Veronica repens*), creeping baby's-breath (*Gypsophila repens*), sweet alyssum (*Lobularia maritima*), and tussock bellflower (*Campanula carpatica*).

Planting along the edge of a path can prevent unwelcome weeds from making a home there.

Occasionally hand-trimming the edges of lawn areas will keep the grass from creeping out over the pavement.

Weeds in Patios and Paving

When you see weeds growing in seemingly impossible places—like the minuscule cracks in an expanse of concrete or blacktop—you get an idea of how tough some plants really can be. There are two ways that weeds find their way into the expansion joints—the cracks—in sidewalks, driveways, and patios. Sometimes they grow up from beneath the crack or from seed that lodges in the crack and sprouts. More often, though, the weeds start in the lawn or the flower bed beside the pavement, then spread along the crack.

You can take steps to prevent weeds from growing in the cracks in patios, driveways, and sidewalks as new pavement is poured. But even if you have an existing paved area, getting rid of weeds that creep in isn't difficult.

Prevention from the Start

If you're having a paved area installed, ask the contractor to put a barrier of heavy landscape fabric or 8-mil black polyethylene—an inexpensive plastic—under the dividers that separate the sections of pavement. As the wood or fiberboard in the expansion joint shrinks over time, the barrier will stop weeds that could come up through the new openings.

Because using barriers isn't a common practice, the contractor might not be willing to do the extra step or may charge more for labor. In that case, you can install it yourself, right before the concrete is poured. The strip of landscape fabric or black plastic only needs to be

Creeping Jenny (*Lysimachia nummularia*) thrives in the cracks between bricks, flagstones, or paving blocks.

about 1 foot (30 cm) wide and centered under the joint.

Another way to prevent weeds is to seal the expansion joint with a urethane caulking made for that purpose. The contractor uses Styrofoam for the expansion joint (rather than wood or fiberboard), then digs out the top 1 inch (2.5 cm) of the Styrofoam before filling the joint with the caulking. This method is expensive and can only be done by contractors because the urethane isn't sold in quantities small

It's easier to control weeds before they get established.

Decorative edging strips are an attractive way to keep plants from spreading out of beds and into paving.

Small weeds such as English daisies (*Bellis perennis*) often seed into the spaces in sidewalks and pavers.

Some pavement plants, such as alyssum (*Lobularia maritima*), are desirable.

A brick edging blends beautifully with most garden plants and helps to keep them from spreading where they're not wanted.

enough for homeowners to buy economically.

One do-it-yourself method that *won't* work is to seal the space in the expansion joints with cement mix or mortar. These rigid materials will crack as the pavement expands and contracts, so all your work will have been wasted.

Controlling Weeds in Cracks

If you didn't or couldn't have a barrier installed in a paved area, you can still keep the weeds in check. Try one or more of these methods:

- Scrape out the weeds with a pavement weeder—a hand tool with a pointed tip that fits into the cracks.
- Pour vinegar, salt water, or boiling water on weeds growing in pavement cracks. Because these materials kill any plant roots they touch, be careful that they don't run down the crack and into nearby plantings. If necessary, you can block the fluid at the ends of the cracks with a rag or piece of cardboard.
- Spray herbicidal soap on young plants. If grass is creeping in from the lawn, you'll probably need to spray more than once. Repeat every week or two as soon as the grass begins to green up again until no new shoots appear.

A sharp-tipped pavement weeder is handy for weeding in cracks.

Stopping Sprawling Grass

Aggressive lawn grasses, such as St. Augustine grass (*Stenotaphrum secundatum*) or bermuda grass (*Cynodon dactylon*), creep onto paved surfaces and can nearly cover them if you don't cut them back regularly. You can edge the pavement weekly with a string trimmer. Or use a manual edger—the kind with a toothed, flat wheel that fits between the lawn and the pavement—every 2 or 3 weeks, before the grass gets too thick and tough to cut. A gasoline-powered edger makes the job easier but not less frequent.

Another way to slow the spread of a creeping grass is to create a barrier. Remove the soil in a strip 2 inches (5 cm) wide and deep between the grass

Use an edging tool to keep a neat edge between grass and pavement.

and the paving to make it a little harder for the grass to spread outward. For extra protection, you can put boards or bricks in the space to keep the soil from filling in and to slow the grass down even more. Or install a flat edging strip that extends down into the soil to block the grass both above and below the ground. Although none of these barriers will completely contain an aggressive grass, they will keep it from taking over the sidewalk as quickly and reduce your routine trimming chores.

Weeds in Neglected Areas

Coping with long-neglected garden areas is one of the most daunting landscaping challenges. Clearing or taming a neglected wooded area, meadow, or garden requires patience, sweat, and—in some cases—loud, heavy machinery. If you choose to forgo the heavy machinery, you increase the amount of patience and sweat required.

Clearing Trees and Shrubs

The first step is to clear out the woody vines, brush, and trees you don't want. If there's just too much growth for pruners and saws to take care of, you can rent any number of machines that will make the task easier. (For a list of your options, see "Bush Whackers.") The type of equipment you need depends on how many woody plants you want to get rid of and how big they are. Whatever you use, be sure to read the instruction manual carefully and follow the safety precautions.

Once you cut down the woody plants, you can use a brush chipper to make your own wood chip mulch. If

Clear weeds around the base of shrubs and trees; then mulch to discourage new weeds from emerging.

the chips are from an evergreen tree or shrub or a black walnut tree, they may contain substances toxic to other plants. Apply them only where you don't want anything to grow (like a pathway). Or let the chips sit for several weeks in an area you don't use, allowing those substances to leach out before you use the chips as mulch around landscape plants.

Depending on how you plan to use the cleared area, you may need to remove the stumps that remain. You can grub out small ones with a pick. For big ones, hire someone with a stump grinder to get rid of them.

Taming the Underbrush

Once you clear out unwanted woody plants, you may be left with a tangle of grasses and broad-leaved weeds. How you handle them depends on what you plan to do with the area and how large the area is. If you want to keep an informal meadow look but want to get rid of some of the species growing there, you can tip the scale in favor of the plants you like. For suggestions, see "Turn Your Weeds into Wildflowers" on page 40.

If you want to turn the meadow into a civilized lawn or garden, you need to clear out the weeds and grasses growing there. If the area is small or if you have plenty of time and energy, you can hoe or dig out the existing plants. Or you can mow them short, then smother them for a couple of months with a dense barrier such as black plastic, old carpet, or cardboard.

brush chipper

Bush Whackers

When you need to clear trees and woody brush from a neglected area, pruners and a saw might not be enough. Here's a rundown of some other equipment you can use yourself or hire a professional to bring in.

- **Weed trimmers** with brush plates have a sawtooth blade that cuts through small trunks 2 to 3 inches (5 to 7.5 cm) thick. They are good for clearing small areas. They are also among the least intimidating tools for people uncomfortable with heavier machinery.
- **Brush mowers** attach to the back of a tractor and cut down the same-size trunks that a weed eater with a brush plate will. But a brush mower takes care of a larger area faster.
- **Chain saws** come in different sizes and can be powered by gas or electricity. Use them to cut down trees.
- **Skid-steer loaders** such as the Bobcat have a loader bucket in front that can push down small trees and dig out their roots.
- **Bulldozers** come in a range of sizes and are useful for pushing trees and brush down and out of the way.

Stinging nettle (*Urtica dioica*) is common in neglected gardens. Mow it repeatedly or smother it with mulch.

If desirable plants spread out of bounds, divide them, replant a few pieces, and compost or give away the rest.

If you have time after clearing or smothering the area, water it and allow seeds and root parts remaining in the soil to resprout. After a week or two, hoe them out again or, for a large area, cultivate with a disc attached to a tractor. If possible, repeat the process once or twice to dramatically reduce the soil's weed supply.

Or, instead of letting the weeds resprout, plant a smother crop. Try two successive plantings of buckwheat during the spring and summer, followed by annual rye in fall. Cut down the smother crop *before* it sets seed. For more details on this technique, see "Choke Out Weeds with Smother Crops" on page 32.

plants, see "Weeds in Ornamental Plantings," starting on page 52.

Once you get the garden cut back and cleaned out, be on your guard for a few years: The soil will no doubt have a good supply of weed seeds and root parts left. Be diligent about mulching, and hoe or pull new weeds as soon as they appear; weeds should gradually become less of a problem.

Reclaiming Old Gardens

Bringing back an old garden requires a softer touch than you get with a bulldozer or even a mower. If woody shrubs and vines have taken over, cut them back to the ground and let them resprout or remove them completely. Dig out any invasive garden plants that have overstepped their bounds. Pull or hoe out weeds, then mulch heavily to keep them from coming back. For specific suggestions on controlling woody weeds and invasive garden

When weeds are out of control, the effect can be overwhelming. Start by mowing flowering weeds before they set seed to prevent the problem from getting worse.

GUIDE TO WEEDS

This handy encyclopedia will help you identify your weeds and then tell you how they grow and how to control them. If you don't know what kinds of weeds you have, you'll find the color photographs an indispensable aid in identifying them. Or, if you think you know what they are, you can look them up by name to confirm your suspicions.

Each weed is listed alphabetically by its botanical name, with its most popular common name clearly shown at the top of the entry. The color photographs highlight key details that help you identify the weed. A detailed description of the distinctive features of each weed—including the leaves, stems, flowers, fruit, and/or roots—and its normal growing range makes correct identification even easier.

The entries also tell you whether the weed is an annual, biennial, or perennial, as well as how it spreads. This information is the basis of the prevention and control methods recommended for each weed.

This guide describes more than 130 weeds. Some are common throughout most of the United States; others are widespread in some areas and rarely, if ever, found in others. If you have an unidentified weed that's not covered in this guide, you may want to ask for help from someone at a local garden center, nature center, botanical garden, or Cooperative Extension Service office.

Before you take a sample for identification, call to find out how you should collect the weed. It's easiest for most plant experts to identify weeds that are intact and not wilted and that have flowers or seed heads (especially for identifying grasses). If possible, dig up and plant the weed in a pot of soil. For weeds too large to pot, cut off a large piece, wrap the stem end in moist toweling, and keep the specimen cool until you can take it to be identified (within a day is best).

If you must mail a sample, press it first. Place it between two sheets of newspaper, then stack several heavy books on the newspaper to press the plant flat. Let it dry for a week or two. To keep the sample intact as it goes through the mail, glue the dry weed to paper (rubber cement is best) and place the paper between two pieces of firm cardboard, then mail. Be sure to include a description of where and when you found the plant and whether you have a few or a lot of them.

Are they garden plants or are they weeds? It often depends on your point of view. Some plants, such as shrubby summer cypress (*Kochia scoparia*), can be attractive in the garden but weedy when they spread out of control.

VELVETLEAF

MAPLES

Velvetleaf is a common annual weed with broad leaves that are covered with soft hairs. Its yellowish late-summer flowers are followed by distinctive fringed seedpods.

OTHER COMMON NAMES: Buttonweed, butterprint, pie marker.

DESCRIPTION: Velvetleaf has an upright stem and floppy, heart-shaped leaves that are covered with soft, velvety hairs. The leaves are 4–10 inches (10–25 cm) wide. The five-petaled flowers are pale yellow to cream-colored and about ¾ inch (18 mm) wide. They bloom in late summer on short stems from the leaf axils (where the leaves join the stem) near the top of the plant. The cup-shaped seedpod is about 1 inch (2.5 cm) in diameter, with a stiff fringe around the edge.

HEIGHT: Velvetleaf normally reaches 4–6 feet (1.2–1.8 m) tall, although it can grow taller.

PREFERRED SITE AND CLIMATE: This weed prefers deep, rich soil. You may find it along fences and in gardens, cropland, and neglected areas. Its range includes the eastern and central Unites States (except for northern Maine, Michigan, and Wisconsin), the Southwest, and the Pacific states.

LIFE CYCLE: Annual.

HOW IT SPREADS: By seed.

SUGGESTED CONTROLS: Mulch the soil to prevent existing seeds from sprouting. Hoe, pull, or flame seedlings as soon as you spot them. Pull, cut, or mow larger plants before they set seed.

COMMENTS: Pioneers pressed the fringed edge of the seedpod into their butter to decorate the blocks.

Maple tree seedlings may pop up anywhere near an established tree—in lawns, hedges, flower beds, groundcovers, potted plants, paving cracks, and even roof gutters!

DESCRIPTION: Maple tree seedlings have lobed leaves that resemble the palm and fingers of a hand; the back of the leaf may be silvery. The seeds are carried in wing-like samaras, which children sometimes call "helicopters."

HEIGHT: Mature maples can grow to 130 feet (39 m) tall, but you'll normally start noticing seedlings when they're just 3 or 4 inches (7.5 to 10 cm) tall.

PREFERRED SITE AND CLIMATE: Most maples grow in the northern and central United States, although there are some southern species. They are found in a wide range of soil and site conditions.

LIFE CYCLE: Perennial.

HOW IT SPREADS: By seed.

SUGGESTED CONTROLS: Regular mowing usually controls seedlings that come up in the lawn. Maple seedlings often sneak into hedges, where you don't notice them until their leaves appear on the outside of the hedge. Pull, cut, or dig out those that sprout in hedges, flower beds, groundcovers, and paved areas as soon as you spot them, preferably before the stems become tough. Once the stems turn woody, you may need to cut the saplings down several times; prune them to the ground every few weeks until new sprouts stop appearing.

Achillea millefolium   Compositae

COMMON YARROW

Common yarrow is sometimes planted for its flowers, but it can spread invasively in average to poor garden soil. Dig out unwanted plants, or smother them with mulch.

OTHER COMMON NAMES: Milfoil, sanguinary, nose-bleed, thousand-seal.

DESCRIPTION: The stems of common yarrow are covered with grayish hairs and tend to branch near the top. The delicate-looking, feathery green leaves are soft and hairy. Flowers bloom in flat clusters all summer and are either yellow or white (or rarely pink).

HEIGHT: Common yarrow is about 6 inches (15 cm) tall in leaf and reaches 1–2 feet (30–60 cm) tall in bloom.

PREFERRED SITE AND CLIMATE: Common yarrow is frequently seen in meadows and neglected areas. It is a common weed on thin, poor soil throughout the United States, except in southern Texas and the Southwest.

LIFE CYCLE: Perennial.

HOW IT SPREADS: By seed and rhizomes (creeping underground stems).

SUGGESTED CONTROLS: Pull, hoe, mow, or cut seedlings as soon as you spot them. Dig older plants to get the creeping roots (let the roots dry out thoroughly before you compost them), or cut the stems to the ground. If you hoe, mow, or cut the plants, you'll need to do it every 1–2 weeks until the roots stop resprouting; or cover the roots with a dense mulch, such as newspaper, cardboard, or plastic. Improving soil fertility discourages yarrow.

Aegopodium podagraria   Umbelliferae

GOUTWEED

Goutweed is a fast-growing groundcover for dry, shady spots where nothing else will grow. In better conditions, it can quickly overtake less vigorous plants.

OTHER COMMON NAMES: Snow-on-the-mountain, bishop's weed, ash-weed, ground ash.

DESCRIPTION: Goutweed leaves are deeply divided. They may be all green or green with irregular white edges. The flower heads are white or yellow, umbrella-shaped clusters that bloom in June. Goutweed grows in patches.

HEIGHT: Goutweed grows 12–14 inches (30–35 cm) tall; the flowers are about the same height.

PREFERRED SITE AND CLIMATE: Goutweed tolerates shade and infertile soil; it will spread more rapidly in moist conditions. It is most commonly found in the eastern United States.

LIFE CYCLE: Perennial.

HOW IT SPREADS: By seed and rhizomes (creeping underground stems).

SUGGESTED CONTROLS: Digging out the rhizomes can reduce the size of a clump, but it's almost inevitable that you'll miss a few rhizomes. Pull, hoe, mow, or cut shoots or existing plants to the ground every 1–2 weeks, until plants stop resprouting. Or cut them back, then cover the area with a dense mulch, such as newspaper, cardboard, or plastic. To keep goutweed controlled as a groundcover, sink barriers at and below soil level.

COMMENTS: If you dig plants, don't toss the fresh roots into the compost pile; spread them out in the sun until they're thoroughly dry to kill them first.

QUACK GRASS

Quack grass spreads easily and requires diligent control efforts. Before composting the rhizomes, lay them out in the sun until they are thoroughly dry.

Yearly tilling will make your quack grass problems worse by chopping up the roots and spreading them through the soil. Try smothering this weed with a cover crop instead.

OTHER COMMON NAMES: Couch grass, quick grass, quitch grass, witch grass. Also known as *Elytrigia repens.*

DESCRIPTION: Quack grass has thin, three- to six-jointed stems that grow in a clump from the base of the plant. The blue-green leaf blades are about ¼ inch (6 mm) wide; they are rough and ribbed on the top, smooth beneath, and pointed at the tip. Glasping auricles—tiny arms of plant tissue that hug the stem at the base of the leaf blade—distinguish quack grass from many other weed grasses. The summer seed head is a dense or loose wheat-like spike of florets; each floret may have a short tail (called an awn) on the end. The rhizomes are extensive, slender, and pointed.

HEIGHT: Quack grass will grow 2–3 feet (60–90 cm) tall if unmowed. In mowed areas, it will adapt to whatever mowing height you use.

PREFERRED SITE AND CLIMATE: This weed makes its home in sunny, open areas such as gardens, pastures, and neglected areas, especially on sites with sandy or gravelly soil. Quack grass grows in all but the most southern states.

LIFE CYCLE: Cool-season perennial; starts growing early in spring.

HOW IT SPREADS: By seed and rhizomes (creeping underground stems).

SUGGESTED CONTROLS: If possible, pull or dig plants, getting as many of the rhizomes as you can. Hoe, mow, or cut shoots to the ground every week or two until they stop resprouting. Or cut them back and cover the area with a dense mulch, such as newspaper, cardboard, or plastic, for at least one growing season. If you can, plant the infested area with a smother crop for 1 year, try two crops of buckwheat (one seeded in the spring, the other that same summer), followed by winter wheat.

COMMENTS: Quack grass spreads easily and requires diligent control efforts. Avoid tossing fresh rhizomes into your compost pile, spread them out in the sun in an out-of-the-way spot until they are thoroughly dry.

| *Agrostemma githago* | Caryophylloceae | *Agrostis palustris* | Gramineae |

CORN COCKLE

Corn cockle is an annual weed with pretty pink flowers and poisonous seeds. Its swollen seed capsule looks like a Chinese lantern encased by ten ribs.

OTHER COMMON NAMES: Purple cockle.

DESCRIPTION: Corn cockle has slender, hairy, narrow leaves that are fused at their base, where they meet the rough, hairy, upright stem. Purple-pink flowers bloom all summer and are borne one per stem. The petals are 1–2½ inches (2.5–6 cm) wide and have distinctive veins; behind them are longer, narrow, green sepals. The seed capsule is inflated, with the sepals at the top. The stems grow from a shallow taproot.

HEIGHT: Plants reach 1–3 feet (30–90 cm) tall.

PREFERRED SITE AND CLIMATE: This pretty weed prefers rocky or gravelly, alkaline soils. You may see it in unmowed areas and in cropland (especially in fields of small grains) throughout the United States; it is particularly common in the Southeast.

LIFE CYCLE: Winter annual.

HOW IT SPREADS: By seed.

SUGGESTED CONTROLS: Mulch to prevent existing seeds from sprouting. Hoe, pull, or flame seedlings as soon as you spot them in fall or early spring. Pull, cut, or mow larger plants before they flower and set seed.

COMMENTS: Corn cockle can be confused with white campion (*Silene alba*), described on page 143, which has white flowers and is found in the northern half of the United States.

MARSH BENT GRASS

Marsh bent grass is grown extensively for top-quality putting-green turf on golf courses, but it's an aggresive spreader that's not suitable for most home lawns.

OTHER COMMON NAMES: Creeping bent grass.

DESCRIPTION: This low-growing grass has narrow, flat, veined leaf blades with rough edges. The stems lie along the ground, then turn upward. There is a tall, rounded membrane at the point where the upper surface of the leaf blade meets the stem. The seed heads form tight, short-branched clusters (panicles) up to 6 inches (15 cm) long.

HEIGHT: Marsh bent grass can grow to 18 inches (45 cm) tall when unmown; in lawns, it grows to whatever mowing height you use.

PREFERRED SITE AND CLIMATE: This grass can adapt to a wide range of site conditions. It is most common in cool, humid regions, such as the northeastern United States.

LIFE CYCLE: Perennial.

HOW IT SPREADS: By seed and stolons (creeping stems).

SUGGESTED CONTROLS: For small patches, pull or dig out as many of the roots and stolons as you can. Pull or dig again every week or two for several weeks to catch shoots that you missed. For larger areas, mow the grass as low as possible, then cover the area with a dense mulch, such as plastic or cardboard, for one growing season.

COMMENTS: If you pull or dig the plants, lay them out in the sun until they are thoroughly dry before adding them to your compost pile.

TREE-OF-HEAVEN

Tree-of-heaven is incredibly tolerant of pollution, and it's sometimes planted on purpose in urban areas where other trees won't grow. It can reseed prolifically.

OTHER COMMON NAMES: Varnish tree, copal tree.

DESCRIPTION: The leaves of this coarse-looking tree alternate along the main stem and are up to 3 feet (90 cm) long. Leaves consist of pairs of leaflets 2–6 inches long (5–15 cm) along the leaf stem; they are toothed near the stem end and have a rank odor when crushed. The early-summer flowers are yellow-green. The fall fruit, a samara, is about 1½ inches (3 cm) long, twisted, and winged.

HEIGHT: Mature trees grow 60–100 feet (18–30 m) tall, though they'll usually be only a few inches to a few feet tall when you notice them growing as weeds.

PREFERRED SITE AND CLIMATE: Tree-of-heaven tolerates tough urban conditions throughout the United States, except in the extreme North. This tree will even grow between cracks in a sidewalk.

LIFE CYCLE: Perennial.

HOW IT SPREADS: By seed.

SUGGESTED CONTROLS: Regular mowing usually controls seedlings that come up in the lawn. Pull, cut, or dig out those that sprout in hedges, flower beds, groundcovers, and paved areas as soon as you spot them, preferably before the stems become tough. Once the stems turn woody, you may need to cut the saplings down several times; prune them to the ground every few weeks until new sprouts stop appearing.

GARLIC MUSTARD

The broad young leaves, white spring blossoms, and slender summer seedpods of garlic mustard are edible raw or steamed. Not surprisingly, they have a garlic flavor.

DESCRIPTION: This garlic-scented plant has an upright and unbranched stem and triangular or heart-shaped leaves with toothed edges. The small, white, four-petaled flowers are borne in clusters from midspring through early summer. The seedpods are short, narrow, and stand upright.

HEIGHT: Garlic mustard grows 1–3 feet (30–90 cm) tall.

PREFERRED SITE AND CLIMATE: This weed tolerates poor, dry soils and is common in shady spots. It is often seen in waste areas and along the edges of woods and roadsides throughout the eastern United States.

LIFE CYCLE: Biennial.

HOW IT SPREADS: By seed.

SUGGESTED CONTROLS: Mulch to prevent existing seeds from sprouting. Seedlings usually appear in fall; hoe, pull, or flame the young plants as soon as you spot them. Pull, dig, cut, or mow larger plants before they set seed. If you cut or mow, check for new shoots a week or two later; repeat the control until no more shoots appear.

COMMENTS: Garlic mustard is sometimes listed in field guides and weed references as *Alliaria officinalis*. The leaves, blossoms, and seedpods are edible raw or steamed; not surprisingly, they have a garlic flavor.

Allium spp.　　　　　　　　　　Liliaceae

WILD GARLIC, WILD ONION

If you dig out wild garlic or wild onion bulbs, don't toss them in your compost pile. Burn them if you can, bury them, or dispose of them with your household trash.

DESCRIPTION: Both wild garlic and wild onion have fleshy, tubular leaves that have a pungent odor. The leaves of wild garlic (*A. vineale*) are long and hollow and hug the stem near the base. Purplish flowers are borne on long stems in late spring through midsummer. Wild garlic produces small bulblets at the top of the stem and underground. The leaves of wild onion (*A. canadense*) are not hollow and are flatter, and they are attached at the base only. Wild onion flowers less often than wild garlic and produces bulblets at the top of the stem.

HEIGHT: Wild garlic grows 1–3 feet (30–90 cm) tall; wild onion grows 1–2 feet (30–60 cm) tall.

PREFERRED SITE AND CLIMATE: Wild garlic and wild onion are often seen in lawns and unmowed grassy areas, especially in humid regions. They tolerate drought and wet soil. Wild onion is more common in the Midwest, wild garlic in the East.

LIFE CYCLE: Perennial.

HOW IT SPREADS: By bulbs and seed.

SUGGESTED CONTROLS: Mow closely or cut plants to the ground every week or two until plants stop resprouting. Or cut them back, then cover the area with a dense mulch, such as plastic, cardboard, or newspaper, for one growing season. In small areas, dig up the plants, getting as many of the bulbs as you can. Improving the soil's drainage can help prevent these weeds from coming back.

Amaranthus spp.　　　　　　　Amaranthaceae

PIGWEEDS

Pigweeds may be annuals, but their prolific seed production can ensure their presence year after year. Control plants before they bloom to prevent reseeding.

DESCRIPTION: Pigweeds are coarse-looking plants with slightly floppy, bristly looking spikes of green flowers in late summer and fall. Both redroot pigweed (*A. retroflexus*) and smooth pigweed (*A. hybridus*) have upright, branched stems; redroot pigweed has a rougher stem than smooth pigweed. Both have oval dull green leaves with a pointed tip. The mature leaves are about 6 inches (15 cm) long.

HEIGHT: Redroot pigweed grows to 6 feet (1.8 m) tall; smooth pigweed can reach 8 feet (2.4 m) tall.

PREFERRED SITE AND CLIMATE: Pigweeds tolerate a wide range of soil conditions. They have made a home in gardens, unmowed areas, and cropland throughout the United States.

LIFE CYCLE: Annual.

HOW IT SPREADS: By seed.

SUGGESTED CONTROLS: Mulch to prevent existing seeds from sprouting. Hoe, pull, or flame seedlings as soon as you spot them. Pull, cut, or mow larger plants before they set seed. Plant a cover crop to smother out heavy infestations.

OTHER SPECIES:

A. albus, tumble pigweed, has stems that spread at the base before turning upward, giving the plant a round shape. When mature, it breaks off at the ground and becomes a tumbleweed that rolls in the wind, dropping its seed as it goes.

Ambrosia artemisifolia Compositae

COMMON RAGWEED

*Although hay fever is often (and unjustly) blamed on the bright flowers of goldenrod (*Solidago *spp.*), *ragweed pollen is the true cause of fall sneezing and watering eyes.*

DESCRIPTION: Common ragweed has an upright, rough, branched stem with fern-like, deeply lobed leaves. The flower heads are green spikes borne at the tips of branches and in the leaf axils (where the leaves join the stem) from midsummer through midfall. The seeds are enclosed in a light brown, woody covering with spines along the top.

HEIGHT: Common ragweed grows 1–4 feet (30–120 cm) tall.

PREFERRED SITE AND CLIMATE: This troublesome weed usually grows in poor, dry soils, but it can adapt to a wide range of soil conditions. It is commonly found in unmowed areas, along roadsides, and in cropland throughout the United States, especially in the eastern and central states.

LIFE CYCLE: Annual.

HOW IT SPREADS: By seed.

SUGGESTED CONTROLS: Mulch to prevent existing seeds from sprouting. Hoe, pull, or flame seedlings as soon as you spot them. Pull, cut, or mow larger plants before they set seed.

COMMENTS: In many states, ragweed is considered a noxious weed and must, by law, be controlled.

OTHER SPECIES:

A. *trifida,* giant ragweed, grows 6–12 feet (1.8–3.6 m) tall. The leaves are divided into three or five lobes. It is most common in moist areas.

Anagallis arvensis Primulaceae

SCARLET PIMPERNEL

Scarlet pimpernel isn't a bad weed; in fact, it looks charming in rock gardens. Consider leaving a few plants to provide shelter and food for some beneficial insects.

OTHER COMMON NAMES: Poor-man's-weatherglass, common pimpernel, shepherd's-clock.

DESCRIPTION: The leaves of scarlet pimpernel are about 1 inch (2.5 cm) long and occur in pairs. They are attached directly to the low, sprawling stem; they have no leaf stems. The star-shaped, ¼-inch (6 mm), white, blue, or scarlet flowers are borne on nodding stems that attach where the leaf meets the stem. They bloom all summer but close during cloudy weather.

HEIGHT: Scarlet pimpernel grows 4–12 inches (10–30 cm) tall.

PREFERRED SITE AND CLIMATE: This weed grows in sandy soil throughout the United States.

LIFE CYCLE: Annual.

HOW IT SPREADS: By seed.

SUGGESTED CONTROLS: Mulch to prevent existing seeds from sprouting. Hoe, pull, or flame seedlings as soon as you spot them. Pull, cut, or mow larger plants before they set seed. Add organic matter to the soil to improve its ability to hold water; this discourages scarlet pimpernel from coming back.

BROOMSEDGE

MAYWEED

Broomsedge is a native perennial meadow grass. It is most noticeable toward the end of the growing season, when its dying leaves turn a reddish brown color.

Mayweed looks somewhat like chamomile, but it's easy to tell the difference when you crush the leaves; mayweed has a distinctive bad odor, while chamomile smells sweet.

DESCRIPTION: Broomsedge grows in a tuft of slightly flattened stems that branch near the top. The leaf blades are 6–12 inches (15–30 cm) long and very hairy on the top side. They turn reddish brown when they dry in fall and winter. The flower head consists of two to four finger-like clusters with tufts of long white hairs that are shielded by reddish brown leaves. Plants bloom from fall through early winter.

HEIGHT: Broomsedge grows 1–3 feet (30–90 cm) tall.

PREFERRED SITE AND CLIMATE: This native grass is a common sight in low-fertility fields throughout the eastern United States and California.

LIFE CYCLE: Perennial.

HOW IT SPREADS: By seed.

SUGGESTED CONTROLS: Mulch to discourage existing weeds from sprouting. Dig or pull plants, or hoe or cut them to the ground every 2 weeks until they stop resprouting. Or cut down the plants and cover the area with a dense mulch, such as cardboard, newspaper, or plastic, for one growing season. Improve soil fertility to keep plants from coming back.

OTHER COMMON NAMES: Common dog fennel, stinking chamomile.

DESCRIPTION: Mayweed has upright, branched stems. The fern-like leaves are finely divided and hairy, and they have a foul smell when you crush them. Small daisy-like flower heads, 1 inch (2.5 cm) or less wide, have a yellow center surrounded by white ray flowers (petals). They bloom from early summer through midfall. Plants grow from a short, thick taproot.

HEIGHT: Mayweed plants can reach 12–18 inches (30–45 cm) tall.

PREFERRED SITE AND CLIMATE: This pretty weed adapts to a wide range of soil conditions. It can pop up in unmowed field and garden areas throughout the United States.

LIFE CYCLE: Annual or winter annual.

HOW IT SPREADS: By seed.

SUGGESTED CONTROLS: Mulch to prevent existing seeds from sprouting. Hoe, pull, or flame seedlings as soon as you spot them. Pull, cut, or mow larger plants before they set seed.

COMMENTS: Mayweed can be a pretty addition to wildflower plantings. It's easy to confuse the leaves with those of common yarrow (*Achillea millefolium*), described on page 85.

HEMP DOGBANE

COMMON BURDOCK

Hemp dogbane has long, narrow seedpods that hang from the plant in fall. They open to release thin, flat seeds with long tufts of hair; these seeds are carried by the wind.

Common burdock is a biennial weed known for its prickly, hooked burs. These burs cling to fur and clothing, providing an easy way for the plant to distribute its seeds.

OTHER COMMON NAMES: Indian hemp.

DESCRIPTION: Hemp dogbane has an upright stem with a woody base and milky sap. The upward-pointing, elliptical, narrow, 2–5-inch (5–12 cm) leaves stand out from the stem at a 45 degree angle and are slightly fuzzy on the underside. Small flowers with five greenish white petals are borne in loose clusters throughout the summer.

HEIGHT: This weed grows 1–2 feet (30–60 cm) tall.

PREFERRED SITE AND CLIMATE: Hemp dogbane tolerates a wide range of soil conditions. You may find it in unmowed areas, along roadsides, and at the edges of woods throughout the United States, except in a band from northeastern Minnesota to central Montana.

LIFE CYCLE: Perennial.

HOW IT SPREADS: By seed and rhizomes (creeping underground stems).

SUGGESTED CONTROLS: Hoe, pull, or flame seedlings as soon as you spot them. Pull or dig larger plants, or hoe or cut them to the ground every week or two until they stop resprouting. Or cut them down, then cover the area with a dense mulch, such as newspaper, cardboard, or plastic, for one growing season.

COMMENTS: Hemp dogbane can be confused with common milkweed (*Asclepias syriaca*), described on the opposite page.

DESCRIPTION: During the first year, the stem of common burdock is short; the second year it elongates, branches, and becomes woody. The large, fleshy leaves are heart-shaped at the base and hairy, especially on the underside. The first-year leaves grow in a rosette near the ground; the second-year ones alternate along the stem, with the largest leaves near the bottom. Small, reddish flowers surrounded by spiny bracts bloom from July through midfall. The seed is a round, hairy bur about ½ inch (12 mm) wide.

HEIGHT: The leafy clumps are about 1 foot (30 cm) tall the first year; plants reach 3–5 feet (90–150 cm) when they flower the second year.

PREFERRED SITE AND CLIMATE: Common burdock grows in fertile, undisturbed soil in the northern two-thirds of the United States.

LIFE CYCLE: Biennial.

HOW IT SPREADS: By seed.

SUGGESTED CONTROLS: Mulch to prevent existing seeds from sprouting. Hoe, pull, or flame seedlings as soon as you spot them. Dig or pull larger plants before they set seed (make sure to get the deep taproot, too). Or cut or mow plants every week or two until they stop resprouting.

COMMENTS: Burdock has round burs, while common cocklebur (*Xanthium strumarium*), described on page 155, has oval ones.

Artemisia vulgaris Compositae

MUGWORT

Don't toss fresh mugwort roots into your compost pile, or you may have a bigger crop of plants next year! Spread them out in the sun to dry thoroughly first.

OTHER COMMON NAMES: Felon herb.

DESCRIPTION: Mugwort has an upright stem and narrow leaves with deep, finger-like lobes. The silvery undersides are covered with fuzzy white hairs. Fragrant, yellow-green flower spikes bloom at the stem tips and in the leaf axils (where the leaves join the stems) from July through early fall.

HEIGHT: Mugwort grows 2–4 feet (60–120 cm) tall.

PREFERRED SITE AND CLIMATE: Mugwort usually makes its home in unmowed areas with alkaline soil in the Northeast and Midwest and in a narrow band along the Pacific coast.

LIFE CYCLE: Perennial.

HOW IT SPREADS: By seed and rhizomes (creeping underground stems).

SUGGESTED CONTROLS: Pull or dig plants, getting as much of the root system as you can. Hoe, mow, or cut shoots to the ground every week or two until they stop resprouting. Or cut them down, then cover the area with a dense mulch, such as newspaper, cardboard, or plastic. Lowering the soil pH by adding sulfur will help to prevent mugwort from coming back in that spot.

Asclepias syriaca Asclepiadaceae

COMMON MILKWEED

Common milkweed spreads by rhizomes and commonly grows in patches. When its seedpods split open, tufts of seeds attached to silky hairs are carried away by the wind.

DESCRIPTION: The upright, stout, fuzzy, unbranched stem of common milkweed is filled with a milky sap. The deep-veined leaves are 4–8 inches (10–20 cm) long and occur in pairs along the stem. Large clusters of fragrant pink or white flowers are borne at the ends of the stems and in the upper leaf axils (where the leaves join the stem) from June through July. The large, teardrop-shaped, gray, hairy seedpods are covered with spines.

HEIGHT: Plants grow 2–5 feet (60–150 cm) tall.

PREFERRED SITE AND CLIMATE: This weed may pop up in woods, along roadsides, and in unmowed spots, especially dry areas. It is found in the eastern half of the United States, except in the Gulf states.

LIFE CYCLE: Perennial.

HOW IT SPREADS: By seed and rhizomes (creeping underground stems).

SUGGESTED CONTROLS: Pull or dig plants, getting as much of the root system as you can. Hoe, mow, or cut shoots to the ground every week or two until they stop resprouting. Or cut them down, then cover the area with a dense mulch, such as newspaper, cardboard, or plastic.

COMMENTS: If you pull or dig plants and roots, spread them out in the sun until they're thoroughly dry before you compost them. Common milkweed can be confused with hemp dogbane (*Apocynum cannabinum*), described on the opposite page.

| *Aster* spp. | Compositae | *Avena fatua* | Gramineae |

WILD ASTERS

WILD OAT

Asters can be weeds if they grow where you don't want them, but they are charming in flower gardens and meadow plantings. They come in a variety of colors and sizes.

Wild oat has a special trick that helps it get established: When the seed gets wet, the "awn" on the seed covering twists and turns, working the seed into the soil.

OTHER COMMON NAMES: Michaelmas daisy, starwort, frost flower.

DESCRIPTION: There are dozens of asters, all of which have small, daisy-like flower heads ½–¾ inch (12–18 mm) wide. The flower heads have yellow centers and may be white, lavender, blue, or pink; they bloom in summer and fall. The stems are upright, branched, and woody. The leaves may be short and thin or large and heart-shaped. The seed has a tuft of hair that lets it be carried on the wind. Some asters have rhizomes and form patches.

HEIGHT: The height varies depending on the species; a typical range is 1–4 feet (30–120 cm), although some species are as tall as 7 feet (2.1 m).

PREFERRED SITE AND CLIMATE: You may see asters in almost any area—along roadsides, at the edge of thickets, in unmowed areas, and in meadows. Some species are even adapted to wetlands.

LIFE CYCLE: Most asters are perennials.

HOW IT SPREADS: By seed; some also by rhizomes (creeping underground stems).

SUGGESTED CONTROLS: Hoe, pull, or flame seedlings as soon as you spot them. Pull or dig larger plants, or hoe or cut them to the ground every week or two until they stop resprouting. If plants are persistent, cut them down and cover the area with a dense mulch, such as cardboard, newspaper, or plastic, for one growing season.

OTHER COMMON NAMES: Tartarian oat, potato oat, flaver, drake.

DESCRIPTION: Wild oat produces smooth, thick stems and narrow leaf blades that are 3–8 inches (7.5–20 cm) long. The late-spring or early-summer flowers hang down from their stems to form a loose, open cluster (panicle). The seed covers have a long spike (called an awn) at one end; the awn is twisted near the base. The plant turns brown by midsummer. Wild oat has an extensive fibrous root system.

HEIGHT: Wild oat grows 1–4 feet (30–120 cm) tall.

PREFERRED SITE AND CLIMATE: This weed can adapt to a wide range of soil conditions. It is a pest in unmowed areas and fields of small grain crops, especially those that aren't rotated to other crops. Wild oat is found throughout the United States, except in the southern third of the eastern states and in the Great Plains states south of South Dakota.

LIFE CYCLE: Annual.

HOW IT SPREADS: By seed.

SUGGESTED CONTROLS: Mulch to prevent existing seeds from sprouting. Hoe, mow, or cut down plants as soon as you notice them to prevent them from setting seed. For infestations in small grains such as wheat, plant other crops in that site for 3 years, cutting down any wild oat plants that appear during that time.

Barbarea vulgaris   Cruciferae

YELLOW ROCKET

Yellow rocket is the first yellow-flowered mustard to bloom in the spring. It produces many tiny seeds that can live in the soil for many years before sprouting.

OTHER COMMON NAMES: Winter cress, rocket.

DESCRIPTION: Yellow rocket has multiple stems that grow out of the crown (the base of the plant near the soil) and branch near the top; these stems may have ridges. Lobed leaves in the rosette at the base of the plant are 2–8 inches (5–20 cm) long. The leaves become less lobed and shorter toward the top of the stems. Bright yellow, four-petaled flowers bloom in clusters at the end of each branch in midspring. The tiny yellow seeds are encased in narrow, 1-inch (2.5 cm) pods. Plants grow from a taproot.

HEIGHT: Plants grow 1–2 feet (30–60 cm) tall.

PREFERRED SITE AND CLIMATE: This colorful weed springs up in moist, rich soil in unmowed areas and along roadsides. It is found in the northeastern United States (as far south and west as Arkansas), in western Washington and Oregon, and occasionally in the northcentral states.

LIFE CYCLE: Short-lived perennial.

HOW IT SPREADS: By seed.

SUGGESTED CONTROLS: Mulch to prevent existing seeds from sprouting. Hoe, pull, or flame seedlings as soon as you spot them. Control larger plants before they set seed in late spring or early summer. Dig or pull them, getting as much of the taproot as possible, or mow or cut plants to the ground every week or two until they stop resprouting.

Bellis perennis   Compositae

ENGLISH DAISY

English daisies can be charming in wildflower plantings or in large areas where you don't need to think about controlling their spread.

DESCRIPTION: The leaves of English daisy form a rosette at the base of the plant and are shaped like a spatula: Narrow at the base and wide and spoon-shaped at the end. The daisy-like flower head is about 2 inches (5 cm) wide and borne at the end of a flower stem that rises above the rosette of leaves. The ray flowers (petals) can be white or pink; they bloom in spring and early summer. Plants spread aggressively.

HEIGHT: The leaves of English daisy usually only grow about 1 inch (2.5 cm) tall, but the flower stem can reach about 8 inches (20 cm) tall.

PREFERRED SITE AND CLIMATE: English daisy prefers moist, fertile soil. It makes itself at home in lawns and neglected areas throughout the United States.

LIFE CYCLE: Perennial.

HOW IT SPREADS: By seed and spreading crowns.

SUGGESTED CONTROLS: Dig or pull plants, or mow or cut them to the ground every week or two until they stop resprouting. Or cut them down, then cover the area with a dense mulch, such as newspaper, cardboard, or plastic, for one growing season.

Bidens spp.   Compositae   *Brassica* spp.   Cruciferae

TICKSEEDS

MUSTARDS

The upright, squarish stems of tickseeds branch near the top and have yellow, daisy-like flowers from summer into fall. The spiked seeds cling to clothing and fur.

Mustard buds, flowers, seeds, and leaves are edible. But unless you plan to eat lots of mustard, control the plants before they go to seed in mid- to late-summer.

DESCRIPTION: Several species of tickseeds are garden weeds. Spanish-needles (*B. bipinnata*) has a square stem that is sometimes hairy. The fern-like leaves grow in pairs on the stem. Flower heads with pale yellow ray flowers (petals) bloom from late summer through midfall. The narrow seeds have four barbed spikes at the end. The stem of devil's beggar-ticks or stick-tights (*B. frondosa*) is slightly hairy and squarish. Each leaf has three or five leaflets that have toothed edges and pointed tips. The flower heads have yellow-orange ray flowers. They bloom from early summer through midfall. The seeds are flat, wedge-shaped, and hairy, with two barbed spines at the top.

HEIGHT: Spanish-needles grows 1–3 feet (30–90 cm) tall; devil's beggar-ticks grows to 4 feet (1.2 m) tall.

PREFERRED SITE AND CLIMATE: Spanish-needles tolerates sandy, rocky, or moist soil in gardens, along roadsides, and in waste areas in the eastern half of the United States, south of central Wisconsin. Devil's beggar-ticks is found in similar areas but is less tolerant of dry soil.

LIFE CYCLE: Annual.

HOW IT SPREADS: By seed.

SUGGESTED CONTROLS: Mulch to prevent existing seeds from sprouting. Hoe, pull, or flame seedlings as soon as you spot them. Pull, cut, or mow larger plants before they set seed.

DESCRIPTION: Common mustards have erect stems, small yellow flowers with four petals, and narrow seedpods. Wild mustard, or charlock, (*B. kaber* var. *pinnatifida*) has a branched stem with a few small hairs near the top. The lower leaves are slightly lobed, with hairy leaf stems (petioles). The smaller upper leaves may be attached directly to the stem. The seedpods are at least 1 inch (2.5 cm) long, with a bent beak at the end. Indian, or leaf, mustard (*B. juncea*) has a hairless stem and deeply lobed lower leaves. The seedpods are 1–2 inches (2.5–5 cm) long, with a cone-shaped tip. Black mustard (*B. nigra*) resembles Indian mustard but has a hairy stem and leaves. The seedpods are ½–¾ inch (12–18 mm) long and cling to the stem.

HEIGHT: Mustards can grow 6–24 inches (15–60 cm) tall, depending on the species and the site.

PREFERRED SITE AND CLIMATE: Mustards adapt to a wide range of soil conditions. You may find them in gardens, grain fields, and unmowed areas throughout the United States.

LIFE CYCLE: Annual or winter annual.

HOW IT SPREADS: By seed.

SUGGESTED CONTROLS: Mulch to prevent existing seeds from sprouting. Hoe, pull, or flame seedlings as soon as you spot them. Pull, cut, or mow larger plants before they set seed. For heavy infestations, control existing plants, then solarize the soil.

| *Bromus* spp. | Grameneae | *Calystegia sepium* | Convolvulaceae |

BROMES

HEDGE BINDWEED

Bromes are grassy weeds that are found throughout most of the United States. They commonly grow in meadows, neglected areas, and rye or wheat fields.

*Hedge bindweed is similar to field bindweed (*Convolvulus arvensis*), except that the leaf lobes on hedge bindweed are squared off instead of pointed, and the flower is larger.*

DESCRIPTION: Bromes have hairy leaf blades and thick, drooping panicles (flower clusters). Japanese brome, or Japanese chess, (*B. japonicus*) has upright stems. The seeds have a ¼–½-inch (6–12 mm) spike, called an awn, at one end. Cheat, or chess, (*B. secalinus*) has upright stems. The leaf blades are only slightly hairy. The awn on cheat is shorter than on Japanese brome or may be absent. Downy brome, downy chess, or cheat grass (*B. tectorum*) has upright or low-spreading stems. The panicle is especially thick, soft-looking, and droopy. The awn is ½–¾ inch (12–18 mm) long.

HEIGHT: Japanese brome and downy brome grow 8–40 inches (20–100 cm) tall; cheat can reach 4–52 inches (10–130 cm) tall.

PREFERRED SITE AND CLIMATE: Bromes adapt to a wide range of soil conditions in unmowed areas and roadsides. Japanese brome and downy brome are found throughout the United States, except in the deep Southeast. Cheat is found throughout the United States, except in Montana, the Dakotas, and Minnesota.

LIFE CYCLE: Winter annual.

HOW IT SPREADS: By seed.

SUGGESTED CONTROLS: Mulch to prevent existing seeds from sprouting. Hoe, pull, or flame seedlings as soon as you spot them. Pull, cut, or mow larger plants before they set seed.

DESCRIPTION: This thin-stemmed vine can trail on the ground or twist around plants and fences. The arrow-shaped leaves have squared-off lobes at the base. White or pale pink, trumpet-shaped flowers are 1½–2 inches (37–50 mm) wide; they bloom from late spring through late summer. The roots are extensive and shallow.

HEIGHT: Hedge bindweed stems can grow 3–10 feet (90–300 cm) long or tall, depending on the site and the height of the support they're climbing.

PREFERRED SITE AND CLIMATE: This troublesome weed pops up in gardens, unmowed areas, cropland, fencerows, shores, and thickets. Hedge bindweed grows in the eastern half of the United States and in Washington and Oregon.

LIFE CYCLE: Perennial.

HOW IT SPREADS: By seed and rhizomes (creeping underground stems).

SUGGESTED CONTROLS: Dig or pull out the young shoots, getting as much of the root system as you can. (Let the roots dry thoroughly in the sun before composting them.) Cut down or hoe plants every week or two until they stop resprouting. Or cut them to the ground, then cover the area with a dense mulch, such as cardboard, newspaper, or plastic, for at least one growing season. For heavy infestations, plant a smother crop for a season or two.

Campanula rapunculoides Campanulaceae

CREEPING BELLFLOWER

Creeping bellflower is sometimes planted for its flowers, but it can quickly creep through and out of flower gardens to become a pesky weed.

DESCRIPTION: The upright, smooth stem of creeping bellflower oozes a milky sap when broken. Heart-shaped leaves with long leaf stems arise from the base of the plant; the upper leaves have short leaf stems or are directly attached to the main stems. The bell-shaped, purple flowers are about ¾ inch (18 mm) long and line the upper part of the stem in late summer.

HEIGHT: This weed grows 1–3 feet (30–90 cm) tall.

PREFERRED SITE AND CLIMATE: Creeping bellflower can tolerate a wide range of soil conditions in lawns, gardens, and fencerows and along roadsides. It is most common in the northern Midwest and Great Plains states, but it may show up in other areas as well.

LIFE CYCLE: Perennial.

HOW IT SPREADS: By seed, stolons (creeping stems), and root fragments.

SUGGESTED CONTROLS: Dig out the plants, getting as much of the root system as you can. (Let roots dry thoroughly in the sun before composting them.) Cut down new shoots every week or two until they stop resprouting. Or cut them to the ground, then cover the area with a dense mulch, such as cardboard or plastic, for one growing season.

COMMENTS: If you really want to grow creeping bellflower for its flowers, surround it with an edging strip or try it in a container.

Campsis radicans Bignoniaceae

TRUMPET VINE

The blooms of trumpet flower are beautiful, but the plant grows rampantly and can become weedy. To control it, prune the previous year's growth back to two or three buds.

OTHER COMMON NAMES: Trumpet creeper, trumpet honeysuckle, cow-itch.

DESCRIPTION: This woody, vining plant has clusters of trumpet-shaped, orange or red flowers from midsummer through midfall. The leaves are 8–10 inches (20–37.5 cm) long and consist of 7 to 11 pairs of leaflets attached along the leaf stem. The seedpod is 4–6 inches (10–15 cm) long, with lengthwise ridges where the pod halves join.

HEIGHT: If uncut, the vines can grow 20–40 feet (6–12 m) long or tall.

PREFERRED SITE AND CLIMATE: Trumpet vine thrives in fertile soil and sun, but it can adapt to less ideal conditions. It grows in gardens, fields, fencerows, and woods and along roadsides in the eastern half of the United States south of Wisconsin.

LIFE CYCLE: Perennial.

HOW IT SPREADS: By seed and rhizomes (creeping underground stems).

SUGGESTED CONTROLS: To get rid of this vigorous, persistent vine, cut the stems back to the ground every week or two until they stop resprouting. Or cut them to the ground, then cover the area with a dense mulch, such as cardboard, newspaper, or plastic, for at least one growing season.

COMMENTS: Trumpet vine is often grown as an ornamental but can become weedy. Prune the vines in spring and dig out unwanted shoots.

Capsella bursa-pastoris Cruciferae

SHEPHERD'S PURSE

Shepherd's purse gets its name from the shape of its seedpods, which resemble the pouches that shepherds carried. This weed is common throughout the United States.

DESCRIPTION: This early weed has a hairy stem and grows upright from a rosette of lobed, dandelion-like leaves at the base. The stem leaves are toothed along the edges and have pointed lobes that clasp the stem. Tiny, white, four-petaled flowers bloom at the ends of the branches from spring into summer. The small, flat, triangular seedpods have a seam along the middle where the two halves join.

HEIGHT: Shepherd's purse grows 1–1½ feet (30–45 cm) tall.

PREFERRED SITE AND CLIMATE: This weed can grow in a wide range of conditions. It comes up in unmowed areas and lawns throughout the United States.

LIFE CYCLE: Annual or winter annual.

HOW IT SPREADS: By seed.

SUGGESTED CONTROLS: Mulch to prevent existing seeds from sprouting. Hoe, pull, or flame seedlings as soon as you spot them. Pull, cut, or mow larger plants before they set seed. For heavy infestations, solarize the soil to kill the seeds.

Celastrus orbiculatus Celastraceae

ORIENTAL BITTERSWEET

Oriental bittersweet is sometimes grown for its berries, which turn orange when ripe. The berries are attractive in arrangements, but they don't make up for this vine's weedy tendencies.

DESCRIPTION: The leaves of this woody, twining vine alternate along the stem and are toothed on the edges. The leaves are narrow near the base and wider toward the tip; the base of the leaf can be rounded or wedge-shaped. Small greenish flowers grow in clusters in late spring through early summer. The flowers are followed by yellow-orange, pea-sized fruits in fall.

HEIGHT: The vines can grow 30–40 feet (9–12 m) long or tall.

PREFERRED SITE AND CLIMATE: Oriental bittersweet adapts to a wide range of conditions. This rampant weed is commonly found along roadsides and the edges of woods in the eastern United States, south from Illinois.

LIFE CYCLE: Perennial.

HOW IT SPREADS: By seed and suckers.

SUGGESTED CONTROLS: Cut the stems back to the ground every week or two until they stop resprouting; persistence is the key. Or cut them to the ground, then cover the area with a dense mulch, such as cardboard, newspaper, or plastic, for at least one growing season.

| *Centaurea* spp. | Compositae | *Cerastium vulgatum* | Caryophyllaceae |

KNAPWEEDS

MOUSE-EAR CHICKWEED

Some kinds of knapweeds are pretty enough to grow in flower beds; others are troublesome weeds. Control them by digging or repeated cutting, or smother them with mulch.

*Mouse-ear chickweed is a common perennial lawn and garden weed. It looks similar to common chickweed (*Stellaria media*) but has hairier leaves and stems.*

DESCRIPTION: Spotted knapweed (*C. maculosa*) has a hairy, branched stem and hairy leaves that are divided into narrow sections. The pink or purple flower heads bloom in late summer and early fall. Russian knapweed (*C. repens*) has a hairy, woody, ridged, branching stem. The hairy leaves near the base are deeply lobed, while those near the top are short and unlobed. The white, light pink, or light blue flower heads bloom from June through October.

HEIGHT: Both species grow to 3 feet (90 cm) tall.

PREFERRED SITE AND CLIMATE: Spotted knapweed prefers dry, gravelly, or sandy soil and is found in the northern two-thirds of the eastern and central United States and in the Pacific coast states. Russian knapweed tolerates moist soil; it grows in the western two-thirds of the United States.

LIFE CYCLE: Spotted knapweed is biennial; Russian knapweed is perennial.

HOW IT SPREADS: By seed. Russian knapweed also spreads by rhizomes (creeping underground stems).

SUGGESTED CONTROLS: Mulch to prevent existing seeds from sprouting. Hoe, pull, or flame seedlings as soon as you spot them. Cut, pull, or mow larger plants every week or two until they stop resprouting, or cut them down and cover the area with a dense mulch, such as newspaper, cardboard, or plastic, for one growing season.

DESCRIPTION: This low-growing plant has fuzzy, little leaves that look like the ears of mice. The leaves attach in pairs directly to the stem, with no leaf stem. The nodes (where the leaves attach to the stem) are often swollen. The thin, hairy stems spread at the base but are upright at the tip. The small, white, spring to fall flowers have five petals that are notched at the tip. The green sepals behind the petals are about the same length as the petals.

HEIGHT: The stems grow 6–18 inches (15–45 cm) long.

PREFERRED SITE AND CLIMATE: Mouse-ear chickweed adapts to a range of soil and site conditions in lawns, pastures, waste areas, and woods. It is found throughout the United States except in North Dakota and in the southern tips of Texas, California, New Mexico, and Arizona.

LIFE CYCLE: Perennial.

HOW IT SPREADS: By seed. It also may root where the lower branches touch the soil.

SUGGESTED CONTROLS: Mulch to prevent existing seeds from sprouting. Pull or cut seedlings as soon as you spot them. Pull or dig out older plants before they set seed, or hoe, mow, or cut the plants to the ground every week or two until they stop resprouting. Or cut them back, then cover the area with a dense mulch, such as newspaper, cardboard, or plastic, for one growing season.

Chenopodium album   Chenopodiaceae

COMMON LAMB'S-QUARTERS

Common lamb's-quarters pops up all over—in flower beds, vegetable gardens, meadow gardens, even container plantings. They grow quickly and can shade out lower plants.

DESCRIPTION: The upright stem of common lamb's-quarters often has green or reddish grooves along its length. The leaves, which alternate along the stem, are egg-shaped or triangular, with toothed edges and a white, mealy coating on the underside. Small green flowers without petals bloom at the ends of the branches and in the leaf axils (where the leaves join the stem) from early summer through fall.

HEIGHT: Plants grow 1–3 feet (30–90 cm) tall.

PREFERRED SITE AND CLIMATE: Lamb's-quarters adapts to a wide range of conditions in gardens and unmowed areas throughout the United States.

LIFE CYCLE: Annual.

HOW IT SPREADS: By seed.

SUGGESTED CONTROLS: Mulch to prevent existing seeds from sprouting. Hoe, pull, or flame seedlings as soon as you spot them. Pull, cut, or mow larger plants before they set seed.

COMMENTS: The young, tender leaves are used as raw or cooked greens.

OTHER SPECIES:

C. ambrosioides, Mexican tea, resembles common lamb's-quarters but has longer leaves with wavy teeth and an unpleasant odor. The leaves also lack the mealy coating.

Chrysanthemum leucanthemum   Compositae

OXEYE DAISY

Oxeye daisy is sometimes grown in wildflower meadows for its cheerful flowers. The plants grow from creeping stems and are usually found in patches.

OTHER COMMON NAMES: White daisy, marguerite, whiteweed.

DESCRIPTION: Oxeye daisy has lobed, dandelion-like leaves along smooth and usually unbranched stems. The typical daisy flower heads have a yellow center with white ray flowers (petals) and are borne one per stem. The flowers are 1–2 inches (2.5–5 cm) wide and bloom all summer.

HEIGHT: Oxeye daisy grows 1–3 feet (30–90 cm) tall.

PREFERRED SITE AND CLIMATE: This pretty weed grows in infertile soil in unmowed areas throughout the United States, except in the northern states of the Great Plains.

LIFE CYCLE: Perennial.

HOW IT SPREADS: By seed and rhizomes (creeping underground stems).

SUGGESTED CONTROLS: Hoe, pull, or flame seedlings as soon as you spot them. Pull or dig larger plants, or hoe or cut them to the ground every week or two until they stop resprouting. Or cut them down, then cover the area with a dense mulch, such as newspaper, cardboard, or plastic, for one growing season.

Chrysothamnus spp.	Compositae	*Cichorium intybus*	Compositae

RABBITBRUSHES

CHICORY

Rabbitbrushes are sometimes grown as ornamentals in dry regions. These much-branched shrubs have long, narrow leaves and clusters of flowers at the branch tips.

Chicory grows from a thick, fleshy, deep taproot. It does not survive in soil that is periodically dug or tilled (such as in a vegetable garden or annual bed).

DESCRIPTION: The branched stems of rubber rabbitbrush (*C. nauseosus*) are covered with woolly gray, white, or green hairs and smell bad when crushed. The stems are densely covered with narrow, long, sometimes woolly leaves. The yellow flowers bloom in round clusters. The seeds have a tuft of hair at the tip. Douglas rabbitbrush (*C. viscidifloris*) is a rounded shrub with upright branches covered with white bark. The brittle twigs may be covered with velvety hairs, and the long, narrow leaves may be twisted and curved. Yellow flowers bloom in broad clusters. The seeds have a tuft of hair at the tip.

HEIGHT: Rubber rabbitbrush grows 1–3 feet (30–90 cm) tall; Douglas rabbitbrush can reach 3 feet (90 cm) tall.

PREFERRED SITE AND CLIMATE: Rabbitbrushes grow in dry, open areas in the western third of the United States, except along the Pacific coast.

LIFE CYCLE: Perennial.

HOW IT SPREADS: By seed.

SUGGESTED CONTROLS: Mulch to prevent existing seeds from sprouting. Pull, hoe, cut, or mow seedlings as soon as you spot them. Pull or dig out older plants before they set seed; or hoe, mow, or cut them to the ground every week or two until they stop resprouting.

DESCRIPTION: This roadside weed has an upright, branched stem that oozes a milky sap when broken. The leaves at the base form a rosette, resembling dandelion leaves; the leaves along the stems are smaller and less lobed. The 1-inch (2.5 cm) flower heads have bright blue, daisy-like ray flowers (petals) and bloom from early summer through late fall. Flowers are borne at the ends of the branches and in the leaf axils (where the leaves join the stem). The flowers close late in the day.

HEIGHT: Plants can grow from 1–8 feet (30–240 cm) tall; they're usually short where they get mowed several times a year.

PREFERRED SITE AND CLIMATE: Chicory grows in fencerows, lawns, and neglected areas with neutral to alkaline soil. It tolerates dry conditions. It is found throughout the United States, except in North Dakota and the Deep South.

LIFE CYCLE: Perennial.

HOW IT SPREADS: By seed and spreading roots.

SUGGESTED CONTROLS: Pull or cut seedlings as soon as you spot them. Pull or dig out older plants (getting as much of the root as possible) before they set seed, or hoe, mow, or cut them to the ground every week or two until they stop resprouting. Or cut them back, then cover the area with a dense mulch, such as newspaper, cardboard, or plastic, for one growing season.

*T*HISTLES

Canada thistle has purple flowers and bristly stems and leaves. Be sure to wear strong gloves to protect your hands when you are working around the spiny plants.

Biennial bull thistle produces a clump of spiny leaves in the first year and spiny flower stems the second year. If you dig out the plants, get as much of the root as possible.

DESCRIPTION: These tall weeds have purple flowers and bristly stems and leaves. Canada thistle (*C. arvense*) has an upright, hairy stem that branches near the top. The slightly lobed leaves have wavy, spiny edges and a silvery under-side. Each branch bears numerous tight, purple flower heads about ¾ inch (18 mm) wide in midsummer through midfall. The leafy bracts beneath the flowers don't have spines. The seeds are attached to tufts of hair that carry them in the wind. Bull thistle (*C. vulgare*) forms a rosette of spiny leaves in its first year, then develops an upright, spiny, sometimes branched stem in its second year. The leaves are spiny like those of Canada thistle but are not silvery underneath. The base of the leaves extends down the stem, creating spiny wings on the stem. The compact pink, reddish, or purple flower head is 1–2 inches (2.5–5 cm) wide. The bracts beneath the early-summer through midfall flowers have spines. The seeds have tufts of hair that carry them in the wind.

HEIGHT: Canada thistle's spiny stems grow 2–5 feet (60–150 cm) tall; bull thistle can reach 3–6 feet (90–180 cm) tall.

PREFERRED SITE AND CLIMATE: Both species grow in unmowed areas. Canada thistle prefers fertile, heavy soil and is found in the northern half of the United States. (It's a common sight in beds of groundcovering junipers!) Bull thistle adapts to a range of soil conditions and grows throughout the United States.

LIFE CYCLE: Canada thistle is a perennial; bull thistle is a biennial.

HOW IT SPREADS: Canada thistle spreads by wind-carried seed and creeping roots. Bull thistle spreads by wind-carried seed.

SUGGESTED CONTROLS: Dig out the plants before they set seed, getting as much of the root system as you can. (Let the roots dry thoroughly in the sun before composting them.) Cut down or hoe new shoots that appear every week or two until they stop resprouting. Or cut them to the ground, then cover the area with a dense mulch, such as cardboard, newspaper, or plastic, for at least one growing season. Be sure to wear gloves when you handle these spiny plants! For heavy infestations, plant a smother crop for a full year or solarize the soil.

POISON HEMLOCK

Poison hemlock was once grown as an ornamental, so you may find it in old gardens. The entire plant is very poisonous when ingested, so use caution when handling it.

OTHER COMMON NAMES: Spotted hemlock.

DESCRIPTION: Poison hemlock forms a rosette of leaves the first year. It produces a tall, upright, branched stem with ridges and purple blotches the second year. The stem is hollow between the leaf nodes. The large, divided, toothed leaves resemble those of parsley. The white flowers bloom in umbrella-shaped umbels at the ends of branches from early summer through early fall. The taproot is long and white and may be branched.

HEIGHT: Plants grow 2–7 feet (60–210 cm) tall.

PREFERRED SITE AND CLIMATE: Poison hemlock may sprout up in fencerows, field borders, and roadsides with fertile gravelly or loamy soil. Poison hemlock is found throughout the United States, except in the northern Great Plains from central Montana to northeastern Minnesota.

LIFE CYCLE: Biennial.

HOW IT SPREADS: By seed.

SUGGESTED CONTROLS: Mow or cut plants to the ground; repeat every week or two until the roots stop resprouting. Or cut them down, then cover the area with a dense mulch, such as newspaper, cardboard, or plastic, for one growing season.

COMMENTS: It's smart to wear gloves when you handle the plants to make extra sure that you don't get the juice on your hands and then in your mouth.

FIELD BINDWEED

Field bindweed is a twining perennial vine that creeps along the ground or wraps around fences and plants. The root system is extensive and deep.

OTHER COMMON NAMES: Creeping Jenny.

DESCRIPTION: This twining vine has arrow-shaped leaves with pointed lobes at the base. The white or pale pink, trumpet-shaped summer flowers are about 1 inch (2.5 cm) wide. They are borne in the leaf axils (where the leaves join the main stems). The flower stalk has two leafy bracts ½–2 inches (12–50 mm) below the flower.

HEIGHT: Vines grow 2–7 feet (60–210 cm) long.

PREFERRED SITE AND CLIMATE: Field bindweed tolerates a wide range of soil conditions. It grows throughout the United States, except in the extreme Southeast, the southern tip of Texas, and southern Arizona.

LIFE CYCLE: Perennial.

HOW IT SPREADS: By seed and rhizomes (creeping underground stems).

SUGGESTED CONTROLS: Dig or pull out the young shoots, getting as much of the root system as you can. (Let the roots dry thoroughly in the sun before composting them.) Cut down or hoe plants every week or two until they stop resprouting. Or cut them to the ground, then cover the area with a dense mulch, such as cardboard, newspaper, or plastic, for at least one growing season.

COMMENTS: Field bindweed resembles hedge bindweed (*Calystegia sepium*), described on page 97, except that the leaf lobes are pointed.

HORSEWEED
DODDERS

Horseweed stems may be sparsely branched or bushy like a horse's tail. To discourage this weed, add organic matter to the soil to help it hold more moisture.

Dodders are parasitic weeds that practically cover their hosts with masses of yellow or orange stems. Spring mulching can discourage existing seeds from sprouting.

OTHER COMMON NAMES: Marestail.

DESCRIPTION: The bristly, upright stem of horseweed usually branches heavily near the top, giving a fan-like appearance. The numerous long, narrow, dark green leaves carry scattered, thick, white bristles. The leaves attach directly to the branch, without a leaf stem. A profusion of flower heads blooms on the upper branches in the leaf axils (where the leaves join the stem). The midsummer through late-fall flowers are greenish with a yellow center and always appear half-open.

HEIGHT: Horseweed grows 1–6 feet (30–180 cm) tall.

PREFERRED SITE AND CLIMATE: This weed commonly grows in dry soil. You may see it in gardens, unmowed areas, and pastures and along roadsides throughout the United States.

LIFE CYCLE: Annual.

HOW IT SPREADS: By seed.

SUGGESTED CONTROLS: Mulch to prevent existing seeds from sprouting. Hoe, pull, or flame seedlings as soon as you spot them. Pull, cut down, or mow larger plants before they set seed.

OTHER SPECIES:

C. ramosissima, dwarf fleabane, is smaller and bushier than horseweed, with fewer flower heads. It is 6–18 inches (15–45 cm) tall. It prefers dry sites in the central and southern United States.

DESCRIPTION: Several species of dodder are garden pests. All are parasites with stringy, yellow or orange, leafless stems that twist around the stems of another plant and send suckers into the stem. The small, white, five-lobed flowers form clusters. Largeseed dodder (*C. indecora*) has coarse stems and usually grows from July to September. Field dodder (*C. pentagona*) has slender stems and grows from spring through fall.

HEIGHT: Dodders form tangled masses of stems of varying height, depending on the height of the plant they're climbing on.

PREFERRED SITE AND CLIMATE: Largeseed dodder prefers moist soil and grows throughout the United States, except in the northeastern quarter. Field dodder favors dry, open sites throughout the United States, except in the northernmost eastern and central states, the northern two-thirds of California, and western Washington and Oregon.

LIFE CYCLE: Annual.

HOW IT SPREADS: By seed.

SUGGESTED CONTROLS: If possible, pull or cut down the host plant before the dodder sets seed, then solarize the soil before replanting in that spot. If you can't remove the host plant, remove as much of the dodder as you can by hand; repeat this several times a season and as needed for the next year or two.

Cynodon dactylon   Gramineae

BERMUDA GRASS

If you have a bermuda grass lawn, keep it out of flower beds with a wide, deep barrier strip. Edge the grass regularly to prevent stems from creeping over the strip.

Bermuda grass can be a tough, vigorous weed when it spreads out of bounds. If you dig the plants out, let the tops and roots dry thoroughly in the sun before composting.

OTHER COMMON NAMES: Devil grass.

DESCRIPTION: This grass has wiry stems that creep everywhere you don't want them to go. Bermuda grass either grows upright or spreads before turning upward. The leaf blades are fine, narrow, and short, with a fringe of hair where the blades meet the stem. The flower heads, which are produced constantly during the growing season, look like thin fingers and bloom at the end of the stem. Bermuda grass has thin, hard, scaly rhizomes underground and flat, creeping stolons aboveground.

HEIGHT: Bermuda grass grows 12–18 inches (30–45 cm) tall when left unmowed.

PREFERRED SITE AND CLIMATE: This warm-season grass prefers sandy soil and is most common in the southern half of the United States.

LIFE CYCLE: Perennial.

HOW IT SPREADS: By seed, stolons, and rhizomes.

SUGGESTED CONTROLS: Pull or dig out unwanted plants, getting as many of the rhizomes as possible. (Let all parts of the plants dry thoroughly in the sun before composting them.) Repeat the process every week or two until plants stop resprouting, or cover the area with a dense mulch, such as newspaper, cardboard, or plastic, for at least one growing season. Solarization can control patches of this grass, but you really need a long, hot, sunny spell to thoroughly heat the soil and kill the rhizomes.

Edge the grass regularly to keep the surface stems from creeping over the mowing stip. Mulching adjacent beds heavily with a coarse mulch also helps to discourage the grass from rooting there.

COMMENTS: Bermuda grass is grown in the South as a lawn and pasture grass. It grows quickly during warm weather and tolerates drought well. Improved hybrids are available for lawns, but they require extra care; they need to be mowed every 5 days during the heat of summer! As a weed, this grass is difficult to control.

| _Cyperus esculentus_ | Cyperaceae | _Datura stramonium_ | Solanaceae |

YELLOW NUTSEDGE

JIMSONWEED

Yellow nutsedge is difficult to control; its shoots can even penetrate thick plastic. Trying to dig out the tubers can spread them and make the problem worse.

Jimsonweed belongs to the tomato family, and it harbors the same insects and diseases that can attack tomatoes, potatoes, eggplants, and other relatives.

OTHER COMMON NAMES: Nut grass.

DESCRIPTION: The glossy, yellow-green leaf blades of yellow nutsedge arise from the base of the stem, which is upright and triangular in cross section. The mid- to late-summer flower head is a loose, yellowish, brush-like cluster (panicle). The plant grows from scaly rhizomes that produce small brown tubers—the "nuts" in the nutsedge.

HEIGHT: Yellow nutsedge grows 8–12 inches (20–30 cm) tall.

PREFERRED SITE AND CLIMATE: Yellow nutsedge is a troublesome weed in gardens, lawns, and fields, especially in wet areas. It is found throughout the United States, except in North Dakota and border areas of adjacent states.

LIFE CYCLE: Perennial.

HOW IT SPREADS: By seed and tubers.

SUGGESTED CONTROLS: Pull out plants as soon as you spot them. The small tubers usually stay in the soil, so keep pulling plants out every week or two until they stop resprouting; be persistent! Mulching with landscape fabric or heavy cardboard for at least one growing season may help to suppress yellow nutsedge; pull out any shoots that come through the mulch. Solarize heavily infested soil.

COMMENTS: If you dig out the tubers, don't compost them; burn them or bury them, if possible, or dispose of them in your household trash.

OTHER COMMON NAMES: Jamestown weed, common thorn apple.

DESCRIPTION: Jimsonweed has large, coarse, toothed leaves that have a foul odor. They are arranged alternately along upright, thick stems that branch heavily near the top. The large white or pink flowers are shaped like a funnel and are 2–5 inches (5–12.5 cm) long. Individual flowers bloom in midsummer through midfall on long flower stalks from the leaf axils (where the leaves join the stem). The spiny, oval seedpod is about 1 inch (2.5 cm) wide. The seeds, which contain toxic alkaloids, are dark, flat, and pitted.

HEIGHT: Jimsonweed can reach 2–4 feet (60–120 cm) tall.

PREFERRED SITE AND CLIMATE: Jimsonweed grows in rich soil in sunny gardens, unmowed areas, and farm fields throughout the East, Midwest, Southwest and along the Pacific coast.

LIFE CYCLE: Annual.

HOW IT SPREADS: By seed.

SUGGESTED CONTROLS: Mulch to prevent existing seeds from sprouting. Hoe, pull, or flame seedlings as soon as you spot them. Pull, mow, or cut down larger plants before they set seed. It's smart to wear gloves when handling the plants, as they may irritate your skin.

COMMENTS: Jimsonweed seeds are poisonous.

QUEEN-ANNE'S-LACE

CRABGRASSES

Queen-Anne's-lace is an attractive biennial weed that often comes up in wildflower meadows, even if it wasn't intentionally planted. The blooms are pretty as cut flowers.

OTHER COMMON NAMES: Wild carrot.

DESCRIPTION: During its first year, Queen-Anne's-lace has a fleshy taproot and a rosette of ferny leaves. During the second year, it produces an upright, thick, hairy stem that branches near the top. The ferny, hairy leaves alternate along the stem; they smell like carrots. The tiny white flowers form flat-topped clusters at the ends of branches from spring through fall; there may be one purplish flower in the center of the cluster. The old flowers curl up and dry, resembling a bird's nest. The small seeds have barbs that cling to fur and fabric.

HEIGHT: Queen-Anne's-lace grows 1–3 feet (30–90 cm) tall in bloom.

PREFERRED SITE AND CLIMATE: This pretty but troublesome weed pops up along dry roadsides and in unmowed areas throughout the United States, except in North Dakota and portions of its adjacent states.

LIFE CYCLE: Biennial.

HOW IT SPREADS: By seed.

SUGGESTED CONTROLS: Mulch to prevent existing seeds from sprouting. Hoe, pull, or flame seedlings as soon as you spot them. Dig or pull larger plants before they set seed (make sure to get the deep taproot, too). Or cut or mow plants every week or two until they stop resprouting.

In garden areas, pull or dig out crabgrass plants before they set seed. In the lawn, raise the height of your mower to shade out crabgrass seeds and seedlings.

OTHER COMMON NAMES: Finger grass.

DESCRIPTION: Several crabgrass species are lawn pests. Large, or hairy, crabgrass (*Digitaria sanguinalis*) has a thick, hairless stem that can be upright or spread on the ground. The leaf blades are usually hairy and ¼–⅓ inch (6–8 mm) wide. The sheaths that surround the stem have a dense covering of long hairs. The flower head is a whorl of three to ten finger-like spikes at the top of the stem. Smooth crabgrass (*D. ischaemum*) is less coarse and shorter than large crabgrass. It also has a purple tinge and is much less hairy. The flower head has two to six spikes.

HEIGHT: Large crabgrass can grow to 3 feet (90 cm) tall; smooth crabgrass can reach 15 inches (40 cm) tall. In lawns both species can adapt to whatever mowing height you use.

PREFERRED SITE AND CLIMATE: Crabgrasses are most common in dry, sandy soil, but they tolerate a range of conditions in lawns, gardens, and neglected areas. Although both species are found throughout the United States, large crabgrass is not in North Dakota and portions of adjacent states, and smooth crabgrass is not in southern Florida, west Texas, and most of New Mexico and Arizona.

LIFE CYCLE: Annual.

HOW IT SPREADS: By seed. Prostrate plants can also root at the stem nodes.

SUGGESTED CONTROLS: Pull or dig up plants before

POORJOE

Repeated mowing encourages crabgrass to grow outward rather than up, so mowing by itself will not control the plants or keep them from reseeding.

Poorjoe is an annual weed that usually grows in dry, sandy soil. It may be found in much of the eastern United States but is most common in the South.

they set seed. Raising the height of your lawn mower (to the upper range that your grass can tolerate) and fertilizing the lawn will help the good grass crowd out this weed. Applying corn gluten meal over the lawn in late spring can kill existing seeds as they sprout; see "Using Herbicides and Boiling Water" on page 70 for more details.

COMMENTS: Repeated mowing encourages plants to grow in a spreading form, so mowing by itself will not control the plants or prevent reseeding.

OTHER COMMON NAMES: Rough buttonweed.

DESCRIPTION: The stem of poorjoe is upright, branched, coarse, and hairy. The rough, narrow, tapered leaves attach in pairs directly to the stem, with no leaf stem. The nodes where the leaves attach to the stem have long bristles. The small, pale pink to lavender flowers bloom at the nodes from early summer through late fall. The seedpods are hairy, with four green teeth at the top, and split in two when ripe.

HEIGHT: Poorjoe grows 8–24 inches (20–60 cm) tall.

PREFERRED SITE AND CLIMATE: This weed comes up in dry or sandy soil along roadsides and in unmowed areas in the eastern half of the United States, except in northern New England and New York.

LIFE CYCLE: Annual.

HOW IT SPREADS: By seed.

SUGGESTED CONTROLS: Mulch to prevent existing seeds from sprouting. Hoe, pull, or flame seedlings as soon as you spot them. Pull, cut, or mow larger plants before they set seed. Discourage the weed from returning by addng organic matter to the soil to help it hold more moisture.

OTHER SPECIES:

D. virginiana, Virginia buttonweed, is a perennial with coarser stems and leaves and larger seedpods.

| *Dipsacus fullonum* | Dipsacaceae | *Echinochloa crusgalli* | Gramineae |

COMMON TEASEL

BARNYARD GRASS

It's easy to identify teasel by its distinctive seed heads. These spiky structures are dramatic in wildflower arrangements and other nature crafts.

Barnyard grass is an annual weed that's common in lawns and gardens throughout the United States. Control it before it sets seed to reduce weed problems the following year.

OTHER COMMON NAMES: Barnyard millet.

DESCRIPTION: Common teasel produces a rosette of leaves at ground level the first year and a coarse, prickly, upright stem the second year. The leaves are long, pointed, and toothed, and they have prickles on the edges. They attach in pairs directly to the stem, without leaf stems. The white or purple, four-petaled flowers bloom in an egg-shaped head that becomes a prickly seed head. It flowers from July through late fall.

DESCRIPTION: The thick, coarse, upright stem of barnyard grass branches at the base. Light green leaf blades are about ½ inch (12 mm) wide. There is neither a membrane nor a fringe of hairs where the inner blade meets the stem. The flower head is a green or purplish, open cluster (panicle) with several branches. The individual florets have short, stiff bristles and a long spike, called an awn, at the tip. Plants bloom from early summer through late fall.

HEIGHT: This weed reaches 2–3 feet (60–90 cm) tall in bloom.

PREFERRED SITE AND CLIMATE: Teasel grows in moist to wet soil along roadsides, ditches, and forest edges in New England and the central Midwest and Great Plains states and along the northern Pacific coast.

HEIGHT: Barnyard grass can reach 1–4 feet (30–120 cm) tall, though it will grow shorter in mowed areas.

LIFE CYCLE: Biennial.

PREFERRED SITE AND CLIMATE: Barnyard grass adapts to a wide range of soil conditions. It grows in yards and gardens throughout the United States, except in the deep Southeast.

HOW IT SPREADS: By seed.

LIFE CYCLE: Annual.

SUGGESTED CONTROLS: Mulch to prevent existing seeds from sprouting. Hoe, pull, or flame seedlings as soon as you spot them. Dig or pull larger plants before they set seed (make sure to get the deep taproot, too). Or cut or mow plants every week or two until they stop resprouting. If the area isn't critical, leave teasel in place to protect sloping soil from erosion.

HOW IT SPREADS: By seed.

SUGGESTED CONTROLS: Pull or hoe plants before they set seed. In gardens, mulch to prevent existing seeds from sprouting.

| *Elaeagnus umbellata* | Elaeagnaceae | *Eleusine indica* | Gramineae |

AUTUMN ELAEAGNUS

The fruits of autumn elaeagnus are popular with birds, and the birds spread the seeds widely. Pull, cut, or dig out the seedlings as soon as you see them.

OTHER COMMON NAMES: Autumn olive, oleaster.

DESCRIPTION: Autumn elaeagnus is a large, wide shrub with oval, pointed leaves that are 1–4 inches (2.5–10 cm) long and silvery on the underside. The stems may be thorny. This shrub bears fragrant clusters of small, yellow-white flowers about ½ inch (12 mm) long in late spring or early summer. Juicy red berries with brown or silvery scales develop in late summer.

HEIGHT: This shrub can reach 18 feet (5.4 m) tall when mature.

PREFERRED SITE AND CLIMATE: Autumn elaeagnus prefers a sunny site with well-drained soil. It grows throughout the United States.

LIFE CYCLE: Perennial.

HOW IT SPREADS: By seed.

SUGGESTED CONTROLS: Pull, cut, or dig out any seedlings that sprout in hedges, flower beds, groundcovers, and paved areas as soon as you spot them, preferably before the stems become tough. Once the stems turn woody, you may need to cut down the saplings several times; prune them to the ground every few weeks until new sprouts stop appearing.

OTHER SPECIES:
E. commutata, silverberry, and *E. angustifolia,* Russian olive, are similar and can also be weedy.

GOOSE GRASS

Goose grass looks very similar to crabgrass. But unlike crabgrass, which has stems that can take root as they spread over the ground, goose grass only grows in tufts.

OTHER COMMON NAMES: Wire grass.

DESCRIPTION: The stem of goose grass spreads flat on the ground in lawns but usually grows upright in unmowed areas. Each leaf blade is 3–12 inches (7.5–30 cm) long and may be rough; it has sparse hairs along the edge. A short membrane splits the blade down the middle where it meets the stem. The flower head is a whorl of two to ten finger-like spikes at the top of the stem; the spikelets on each spike join in a zipper-like pattern.

HEIGHT: The stems can grow 6–24 inches (15–60 cm) tall, but they can adapt to whatever mowing height you use for your lawn.

PREFERRED SITE AND CLIMATE: Goose grass adapts to a range of soil conditions. It grows in lawns, gardens, roadsides, and neglected areas throughout the United States, except in northern Maine, Wisconsin, the Dakotas, and the northern Great Plains states.

LIFE CYCLE: Annual.

HOW IT SPREADS: By seed.

SUGGESTED CONTROLS: Mulch to prevent existing seeds from sprouting. Hoe, pull, or flame seedlings as soon as you spot them. Pull out or cut down larger plants before they set seed.

COMMENTS: Goose grass resembles large crabgrass (*Digitaria sanguinalis*), described on page 108, but has darker leaves and grows only in tufts.

Equisetum arvense Equisetaceae	*Erigeron annuus* Compositae

FIELD HORSETAIL

ANNUAL FLEABANE

Digging out the creeping stems of field horsetail can reduce the size of a clump, but it's almost inevitable that you'll miss a few rhizomes and have new shoots coming up.

Annual fleabane produces daisy-like white or lavender flowers through most of the growing season. The seeds have tufts of hair that carry them on the wind.

OTHER COMMON NAMES: Horsetail fern, scouring rush.

DESCRIPTION: Field horsetail is a primitive plant with large, jointed stems and a fruiting head that looks like a pinecone. The wiry, tough, hollow stems may be vegetative (not bearing flowers) or fertile. Vegetative stems produce a whorl of branches at each node (stem joint). Fertile stems are unbranched, with prominent swollen nodes and a fruiting head at the tip. Vegetative stems appear from spring through frost; fertile stems bloom in late spring. The fruiting head resembles a small pinecone and is full of spores. Horsetail often grows in patches.

HEIGHT: This weed grows to 18 inches (45 cm) tall.

PREFERRED SITE AND CLIMATE: Field horsetail grows in moist conditions, especially in sandy or gravelly soil. It is found throughout the United States, except in the Southeast.

LIFE CYCLE: Perennial.

HOW IT SPREADS: By spores and rhizomes (creeping underground stems).

SUGGESTED CONTROLS: Pull, hoe, mow, or cut shoots to the ground every 1–2 weeks until they stop resprouting. Or cut them back, then cover the area with a dense mulch, such as landscape fabric, cardboard, or plastic, for at least one growing season. Frequent tilling or digging will discourage the weed from returning.

OTHER COMMON NAMES: Daisy fleabane, white top, sweet scabious.

DESCRIPTION: Annual fleabane has an upright stem that is branched near the top and may have scattered stiff hairs. Lower leaves are larger and more toothed along the margins than those near the top. The upper leaves are small and taper sharply toward the leaf base. The daisy-like flower head is ½–1 inch (12–25 mm) wide and has white or pale purple ray flowers (petals) and a yellow center. Plants bloom from late spring through late fall.

HEIGHT: This weed grows 1–3 feet (30–90 cm) tall.

PREFERRED SITE AND CLIMATE: Annual fleabane tolerates a range of soil conditions. It is found in fields, roadsides, and neglected areas in the eastern half of the United States (except in the deep Southeast), along the Pacific coast, and in northern Idaho and western Montana.

LIFE CYCLE: Annual, winter annual, or biennial.

HOW IT SPREADS: By seed.

SUGGESTED CONTROLS: Mulch to prevent existing seeds from sprouting. Hoe, pull, or flame seedlings as soon as you spot them. Dig or pull larger plants before they set seed, getting as much of the root system as you can. Or cut or mow plants every week or two until they stop resprouting.

COMMENTS: Fleabanes are said to repel fleas—hence the name.

| *Erodium cicutarium* | Geraniaceae | *Euphorbia corollata* | Euphorbiaceae |

REDSTEM FILAREE

FLOWERING SPURGE

Redstem filaree is a low-growing annual or biennial weed that thrives in dry soil. If you dig or pull out the plants, try to get the taproot too to prevent resprouting.

OTHER COMMON NAMES: Storksbill, filaria, wild musk, pin clover, pin grass.

DESCRIPTION: The fern-like leaves of redstem filaree often form a rosette that lies flat on the ground. Pink, five-petaled flowers that are less than ½ inch (12 mm) wide bloom from spring through fall. The seedpod ends in a beak that resembles a crane's bill.

HEIGHT: Plants may be 3–12 inches (7.5–30 cm) tall.

PREFERRED SITE AND CLIMATE: Redstem filaree usually grows along sandy roadsides and in neglected areas in the northcentral and northeastern United States, including the Great Plains.

LIFE CYCLE: Winter annual or biennial.

HOW IT SPREADS: By seed.

SUGGESTED CONTROLS: Mulch to prevent existing seeds from sprouting. Hoe, pull, or flame seedlings as soon as you spot them. Dig or pull larger plants before they set seed. Or cut or mow plants every week or two until they stop resprouting.

COMMENTS: The flowers and seedpods of redstem filaree resemble those of Carolina geranium (*Geranium carolinianum*), described on page 116, but the leaves are fern-like instead of shaped like the palm of a hand.

Flowering spurge is a pretty weed that's sometimes grown in flower beds or prairie gardens. The small flowers are surrounded by a cup of five bracts that look like petals.

OTHER COMMON NAMES: Tramp's spurge, wild hippo.

DESCRIPTION: The upright, light green stem of flowering spurge is branched near the top and oozes a milky sap when broken. The lower leaves are narrow and oblong, and they alternate along the stem. The upper leaves are smaller and form a circle, or whorl, around the stem. The white flowers are borne at the ends of branches and in the leaf axils (where the leaves join the stem) from early summer through midfall. The seedpods have short stalks and are three-sided.

HEIGHT: This weed grows 1–3 feet (30–90 cm) tall.

PREFERRED SITE AND CLIMATE: Flowering spurge is often seen along dry or sandy roadsides and unmowed areas in the eastern half of the United States, except in the most northern states.

LIFE CYCLE: Perennial.

HOW IT SPREADS: By seed and short rhizomes (creeping underground stems).

SUGGESTED CONTROLS: Pull, hoe, mow, or cut seedlings as you spot them. Dig older plants to get the roots (let the roots dry thoroughly before you compost them), or cut the stems to the ground. If you hoe, mow, or cut the plants, do it every 1–2 weeks until the roots stop resprouting. Or cover the roots with a dense mulch, such as newspaper or cardboard, for one growing season.

| *Euphorbia cyparissias* | Euphorbiaceae | *Euphorbia nutans* | Euphorbiaceae |

CYPRESS SPURGE

NODDING SPURGE

If you grow cypress spurge as a groundcover, surround it with barrier strips to keep it from spreading out of control. It can easily escape from gardens and become weedy.

Nodding spurge has reddish, upright stems that are filled with a milky sap. This annual is a common garden weed throughout the United States.

DESCRIPTION: Cypress spurge has leafy stems that release a milky sap when broken. The sprawling stems form dense mats that lie flat on the ground. Long, narrow, pale green leaves alternate along the stem. Plants bloom in spring and summer. The small, greenish flowers have fused petals that form a cup; they grow at the ends of the branches in a whorl of petal-like bracts. The bracts turn from yellow to purplish as they age. The flowers are followed by three-sided, waxy seedpods that grow on short stems.

HEIGHT: Branches can grow to 1 foot (30 cm) long.

PREFERRED SITE AND CLIMATE: This weed is usually found in dry, sandy soil in yards and neglected areas and along roadsides in the eastern United States.

LIFE CYCLE: Perennial.

HOW IT SPREADS: Usually by rhizomes (creeping underground stems), but sometimes by seed.

SUGGESTED CONTROLS: Pull, hoe, mow, or cut seedlings as soon as you spot them. Dig older plants to get the creeping roots (let the roots dry out thoroughly before you compost them), or cut the stems to the ground. If you hoe, mow, or cut the plants, you'll need to do it again every 1–2 weeks until the roots stop resprouting. Or cover the roots with a dense mulch, such as newspaper, cardboard, or plastic, for at least one growing season.

DESCRIPTION: The reddish, upright stem of spotted spurge has branches that spread out and are filled with a milky sap. The oval leaves are ¾–1 inch (18–25 mm) long, with tiny teeth on the edges and a red spot in the center. The early-summer through fall flowers are small, with tiny cupped petals.

HEIGHT: Plants grow 6–36 inches (15–90 cm) tall.

PREFERRED SITE AND CLIMATE: Nodding spurge adapts to a wide range of soil conditions. It is found in gardens and neglected areas throughout the United States.

LIFE CYCLE: Annual.

HOW IT SPREADS: By seed.

SUGGESTED CONTROLS: Mulch to prevent existing seeds from sprouting. Hoe, pull, or flame seedlings as soon as you spot them. Pull, cut, or mow larger plants before they set seed.

OTHER SPECIES:

E. maculata, spotted spurge (also called milk purslane), has hairier, smaller leaves. The purplish stem has milky sap and forms a mat that lies flat on the ground. It is common in lawns and can be confused with prostrate knotweed (*Polygonum aviculare*), described on page 133.

Galinsoga parviflora   Compositae

SMALLFLOWER GALINSOGA

Smallflower galinsoga is a pesky annual weed that often pops up in vegetable gardens. Control plants as soon as you spot them; the tiny flowers can quickly go to seed.

DESCRIPTION: The slender, slightly hairy stem of smallflower galinsoga has many branches and can be upright or spreading. The thin, toothed, pointed leves grow along the stem in pairs. The many small flower heads resemble tiny daisies that are missing half of their petals. Each flower head is made up of four or five widely spaced, tiny, white ray flowers (petals) surrounding a yellow center. They bloom from early summer through late fall.

HEIGHT: This common weed grows 1–2 feet (30–60 cm) tall.

PREFERRED SITE AND CLIMATE: Smallflower galinsoga is a troublesome weed in gardens and unmowed areas with moist, rich soil. It is found throughout the United States, except along the central Atlantic coast and in the most northern states.

LIFE CYCLE: Annual.

HOW IT SPREADS: By seed.

SUGGESTED CONTROLS: Mulch to prevent existing seeds from sprouting. Hoe, pull, or flame seedlings as soon as you spot them. Pull, cut, or mow larger plants before they set seed.

OTHER SPECIES: *G. ciliata*, hairy galinsoga, is similar but hairier.

Galium spp.   Rubiaceae

BEDSTRAWS

Catchweed bedstraw spreads by small, spiny seeds that stick tenaciously to fur and fabric. The edges of its four-sided stem have a row of short, stiff bristles.

DESCRIPTION: Several bedstraw species can be garden pests. Catchweed bedstraw (*G. aparine*) has long, weak stems that flop over onto the ground. The edges of the four-sided stem have a row of short, stiff bristles that point downward. Narrow, rough, bristly leaves form circles or whorls around the stem. From late spring through midsummer, small, white, four-petaled flowers bloom on thin stems that extend from the whorl of leaves. The seed is a bur that looks like two tiny eggs stuck together and is covered with spines. Smooth or white bedstraw (*C. mollugo*), also known as false baby's breath, is similar but has smaller, shorter leaves. The stem may be hairy but isn't prickly.

HEIGHT: The stems of catchweed bedstraw are 1–3 feet (30–90 cm) long. Smooth bedstraw stems can grow as long as 4 feet (1.2 m).

PREFERRED SITE AND CLIMATE: Catchweed bedstraw is found in moist woods, thickets, roadsides, and unmowed areas throughout the United States. Smooth bedstraw is found on gravelly or sandy soil along the central and northern coast of California and the southern coast of Oregon and in northern New England west to southern Indiana.

BEDSTRAWS—CONTINUED

CAROLINA GERANIUM

Smooth or white bedstraw is a perennial weed that spreads by seed and creeping underground stems. Cut, pull, or dig plants repeatedly, or smother the roots with a dense mulch.

LIFE CYCLE: Catchweed bedstraw is an annual; smooth bedstraw is a perennial.

HOW IT SPREADS: By seed that sticks to fur and fabric. Smooth bedstraw also has rooting stems and rhizomes (creeping underground stems).

SUGGESTED CONTROLS: Mulch to prevent existing seeds from sprouting. Pull, hoe, mow, or cut seedlings as soon as you spot them. Mow, hoe, or pull older plants of catchweed bedstraw before they set seed. Dig older plants of smooth bedstraw to get the creeping roots (let the roots dry out thoroughly before you compost them), or cut the stems to the ground. If you hoe, mow, or cut the plants, you'll need to do it again every 1–2 weeks until the roots stop resprouting. Or cover the roots with a dense mulch, such as newspaper, cardboard, or plastic, for one growing season.

COMMENTS: The burs stick tenaciously to shoelaces and socks.

The small pink or lavender flowers of Carolina geranium are followed by long, pointed seedpods. The mature seedpods split into five sections and scatter the seeds.

OTHER COMMON NAMES: Carolina cranesbill.

DESCRIPTION: Carolina geranium has an upright stem that branches near the base. The lobed leaves are 1–3 inches (2.5–7.5 cm) wide and resemble the palm and fingers of a hand. Small, five-petaled, pale pink to purple flowers bloom singly or in clusters on the ends of stems from late spring through midsummer. When mature, the long, pointed seedpod splits into five curled sections.

HEIGHT: Carolina geranium grows 4–20 inches (10–50 cm) tall.

PREFERRED SITE AND CLIMATE: Look for this pretty weed in dry or sandy lawns, woods, and neglected areas and along roadsides throughout the United States.

LIFE CYCLE: Annual.

HOW IT SPREADS: By seed.

SUGGESTED CONTROLS: Mulch to prevent existing seeds from sprouting. Hoe, pull, or flame seedlings as soon as you spot them. Pull, cut, or mow larger plants before they set seed.

Glechoma hederacea   Labiatae

GROUND IVY

Ground ivy is a tenacious perennial weed that spreads by seed and creeping stems. Controlling this weed in lawns and flower beds demands persistence.

OTHER COMMON NAMES: Creeping Charlie, gill-over-the-ground, runaway robin, field balm, alehoof.

DESCRIPTION: The four-sided stem of ground ivy creeps close to the ground, rooting at the nodes (stem joints). Circular or kidney-shaped, bright green, hairy leaves are ½–1½ inches (12–37 mm) wide and have wavy, rounded edges. The small, blue, trumpet-shaped flowers have two lips. They bloom in mid- to late-spring in the leaf axils (where the leaves join the stem).

HEIGHT: The stems are 15–30 inches (37–75 cm) long.

PREFERRED SITE AND CLIMATE: Ground ivy grows in lawns, orchards, and neglected areas, especially in shady areas with rich, moist soil. It is found in the eastern half of the United States, except in Florida and southern Georgia.

LIFE CYCLE: Perennial.

HOW IT SPREADS: By seed and creeping stems.

SUGGESTED CONTROLS: Fertilize lawns to help the grass compete with this agressive weed. Pull or hoe plants often. For heavy infestations (where the lawn has been choked out), cut or mow the plants close to the ground, then cover the area with a dense mulch, such as cardboard, newspaper, or plastic, for one growing season.

Helianthus annuus   Compositae

COMMON SUNFLOWER

Common sunflower often pops up under bird feeders and in nearby gardens and groundcovers. You might consider leaving a few seedlings to grow if they're not in the way.

OTHER COMMON NAMES: Wild sunflower.

DESCRIPTION: Common sunflower can be identified before it blooms by its large, rough, pointed, teardrop-shaped leaves with a sawtoothed edge. The leaves alternate along the upright, thick, rough stem. The lower leaves have a longer leaf stem than the upper ones. From midsummer through late fall, common sunflower bears flower heads that are 1–5 inches (2.5–12.5 cm) wide, with a reddish brown center and yellow ray flowers (petals). The gray to black seeds are ⅛–¼ inch (3–6 mm) long.

HEIGHT: Common sunflower can grow 2–10 feet (60–300 cm) tall.

PREFERRED SITE AND CLIMATE: Common sunflower adapts to a range of soil conditions. You may see it along roadsides and in unmowed areas throughout the United States.

LIFE CYCLE: Annual.

HOW IT SPREADS: By seed.

SUGGESTED CONTROLS: Mulch to prevent existing seeds from sprouting. Hoe, pull, or flame seedlings as soon as you spot them. Pull, cut, or mow larger plants before they set seed.

COMMENTS: Common sunflowers look appropriate in wildflower plantings and will attract birds to your garden.

Hieracium spp.   Compositae

HAWKWEEDS

If you dig out hawkweed roots, let them dry thoroughly before composting them. Improving the soil's fertility with organic matter can discourage hawkweeds from returning.

DESCRIPTION: Two species of hawkweed are trouble-some garden weeds. Orange hawkweed, devil's paintbrush, or king-devil (*H. aurantiacum*) has an upright, leafless, hairy stem that oozes a milky sap when broken. The long, narrow, hairy leaves form a rosette near the ground. Flower heads less than 1 inch (2.5 cm) wide bloom at the top of the stem and have orange ray flowers (petals). Yellow hawkweed (*H. pratense*) is similar to orange hawkweed but has yellow flower heads and black hairs near the top of the stem.

HEIGHT: Orange hawkweed grows 6–18 inches (15–45 cm) tall; yellow hawkweed reaches 6–36 inches (15–90 cm) tall.

PREFERRED SITE AND CLIMATE: Both species are found in infertile unmowed areas, mostly in the eastern United States.

LIFE CYCLE: Perennial.

HOW IT SPREADS: By seed. Orange hawkweed has stolons; yellow hawkweed has rhizomes and some-times also produces stolons.

SUGGESTED CONTROLS: Pull, hoe, mow, or cut seed-lings as soon as you spot them. Dig older plants to get the roots, or cut the stems to the ground. If you hoe, mow, or cut the plants, do it again every 1–2 weeks until the roots stop resprouting. Or cover the roots with a dense mulch, such as cardboard or plastic, for one growing season.

Holcus lanatus   Gramineae

COMMON VELVET GRASS

Common velvet grass is a perennial weed with soft, hairy leaves. This summer-blooming grass is usually found in the northern United States.

DESCRIPTION: Common velvet grass has grayish stems with pinkish ridges and flat, pointed leaf blades covered with thick, velvety hairs. A membranous piece of tissue with a jagged rim and hairs on the back is found where the leaf blade meets the stem. The seed head is a plume-like panicle that's 2–5 inches (5–12.5 cm) long. The individual spikelets have a short, soft awn (spine-like extension).

HEIGHT: This grassy weed grows to 3 feet (90 cm) tall.

PREFERRED SITE AND CLIMATE: Common velvet grass is found in sandy soil in fields and along roadsides in the northern half of the United States, especially in the Pacific Northwest.

LIFE CYCLE: Perennial.

HOW IT SPREADS: By seed and rhizomes (creeping underground stems).

SUGGESTED CONTROLS: Dig plants to get the creep-ing roots (let the roots dry out thoroughly before you compost them), or cut the stems to the ground. If you hoe, mow, or cut the plants, you'll need to do it again every 1–2 weeks until the roots stop resprouting. Or cover the roots with a dense mulch, such as newspaper, cardboard, or plastic, for one growing season. To discourage plants from return-ing, add organic matter to increase the soil's ability to hold moisture.

| *Hordeum jubatum* | Gramineae | *Hypericum perforatum* | Guttiferae |

FOXTAIL BARLEY

ST.-JOHN'S-WORT

Foxtail barley is sometimes grown in flower beds or meadow gardens for its showy seed heads. Mow plants after bloom if you don't want them to reseed.

St.-John's-wort, also commonly known as klamath weed, is a perennial weed with yellow summer flowers. It spreads by seed and creeping roots and is difficult to control.

OTHER COMMON NAMES: Wild barley, squirreltail barley, squirreltail grass.

DESCRIPTION: Foxtail barley has leaf blades that are ⅛–¼ inch (3–6 mm) wide and rough on the upper surface. The leaf blades alternate along the upright, clump-forming stems. The drooping flower head is a spike, 2–5 inches (5–12.5 cm) long, with soft, yellow or purplish bristles about 2 inches (5 cm) long.

HEIGHT: Foxtail barley grows 1–2 feet (30–60 cm) tall.

PREFERRED SITE AND CLIMATE: This grassy weed tolerates a wide range of soil conditions. It grows along roadsides and pastures throughout the United States, except in the Southeast and eastern Texas.

LIFE CYCLE: Perennial.

HOW IT SPREADS: By seed.

SUGGESTED CONTROLS: Dig plants to get the roots, or cut the stems to the ground. If you hoe, mow, or cut the plants, do it again every 1–2 weeks until the roots stop resprouting. Or cover the roots with a dense mulch, such as newspaper, cardboard, or plastic, for at least one growing season.

OTHER SPECIES:
   H. murimum, another species commonly called foxtail barley, is an annual with a similar seed head, but its stems lie flat on the ground rather than growing upright.

OTHER COMMON NAMES: Klamath weed.

DESCRIPTION: St.-John's-wort has oblong leaves covered with tiny pinholes that let the light through. The leaves attach directly to the upright, branched stem that has a woody base. Plants bloom all summer, bearing flowers that are about ¾ inch (18 mm) wide. Each flower has five yellow-orange petals with dark dots at the edge. The round seedpods have a pointed tip.

HEIGHT: St.-John's-wort grows 1–2 feet (30–60 cm) tall.

PREFERRED SITE AND CLIMATE: This weed is common in dry, unmowed areas and along roadsides in the eastern half of the United States and the Pacific Northwest.

LIFE CYCLE: Perennial.

HOW IT SPREADS: By seed and creeping roots.

SUGGESTED CONTROLS: Mulch to prevent existing seeds from sprouting. Dig plants to get the roots, or cut the stems to the ground. If you hoe, mow, or cut the plants, do it again every 1–2 weeks until the roots stop resprouting. Or cover the roots with a dense mulch, such as newspaper, cardboard, or plastic, for at least one growing season.

COMMENTS: St.-John's-wort contains a chemical that irritates the mouths of livestock and may make white animals have an allergic reaction to sunlight.

| *Impatiens* spp. | Balsaminaceae | *Ipomoea* spp. | Convolvulaceae |

TOUCH-ME-NOTS

MORNING GLORIES

Touch-me-nots are common in moist, shady sites but usually aren't a real problem. Their stems contain a juicy sap that can relieve the itching caused by poison ivy or nettle stings.

If morning glory vines wrap around plants that you want to save, trace the weed stems back to the ground before pulling or cutting them; then carefully untangle the tops.

DESCRIPTION: Several species of *Impatiens* are planted for their pretty flowers; a few species are vigorous enough to become weeds. Pale touch-me-not (*I. pallida*) has an upright stem that oozes a watery sap when broken. The oval leaves have a pointed tip and scalloped edges. Plants bear pale yellow, drooping flowers from midsummer through early fall; each flower has a short spur. The ripe seedpod explodes when touched. Spotted touch-me-not, or snapweed (*I. capensis*), is similar to pale touch-me-not, but the flower is orange and has a longer spur.

HEIGHT: Both species can grow 3–5 feet (90–150 cm) tall.

PREFERRED SITE AND CLIMATE: Touch-me-nots thrive in wet, shady places where the soil is high in calcium. They grow in the eastern United States, as far south and west as Kansas.

LIFE CYCLE: Annual.

HOW IT SPREADS: By seed.

SUGGESTED CONTROLS: Mulch to prevent existing seeds from sprouting. Hoe, pull, or flame seedlings as soon as you spot them. Pull, cut, or mow larger plants before they set seed. To discourage plants from returning, add sulfur to counteract the calcium, and add organic matter to improve drainage.

DESCRIPTION: Morning glories have beautiful flowers, but they can also be pesky garden weeds. The hairy leaves of both ivy-leaved morning glory (*I. hederacea*) and tall morning glory (*I. purpurea*) alternate along hairy, vining stems. The leaves of ivy-leaved morning glory have three deep lobes; the leaves of tall morning glory are heart-shaped. The trumpet-shaped flowers are usually purple, pink, blue, or bluish white. Both species bloom from midsummer through midfall.

HEIGHT: The vines of both species can be 6–10 feet (1.8–3 m) long.

PREFERRED SITE AND CLIMATE: Morning glories adapt to a range of soil conditions along roadsides and in gardens and unmowed areas. Ivy-leaved morning glory grows in the eastern half of the United States (except in the most northern states), the central Great Plains states, and the Southwest. Tall morning glory grows in the eastern half of the United States, except in northern Wisconsin, Minnesota, and the Dakotas. It also grows along the Pacific coast.

LIFE CYCLE: Annual.

HOW IT SPREADS: By seed.

SUGGESTED CONTROLS: Mulch to prevent existing seeds from sprouting. Hoe, pull, or flame seedlings as soon as you spot them. Pull, cut, or mow larger plants before they set seed.

Juniperus virginiana　　　　　Cupressaceae

EASTERN RED CEDAR

Eastern red cedars are a common sight in neglected farm fields and roadsides. They spread quickly in areas that are not subject to mowing or fires.

DESCRIPTION: This evergreen tree may be tall and narrow or short and wide. The bark is reddish brown and hangs on the trunk in loose strips. Trees usually have two types of needles: wide ones made up of scales and narrow, prickly ones. The fruit is a blue berry.

HEIGHT: Mature trees can grow to 75 feet (21 m) tall.

PREFERRED SITE AND CLIMATE: Eastern red cedar adapts to a range of soil conditions, including poor, dry soil. It may pop up in flower and groundcover beds; it's especially common in unmowed areas. This tree grows throughout much of the United States.

LIFE CYCLE: Perennial.

HOW IT SPREADS: By seed.

SUGGESTED CONTROLS: Pull, mow, cut, or flame seedlings as soon as you spot them. Cut undesired older adult trees to the ground; they usually don't resprout.

COMMENTS: Eastern red cedar pollen causes hay fever in many people. It is a host for cedar-apple rust, a fungal disease that is usually harmless to eastern red cedar but a problem for apple trees. The berry is used to make gin.

Kochia scoparia　　　　　Chenopodiaceae

SUMMER CYPRESS

Summer cypress is occasionally grown in gardens for its handsome, shrubby form and bright red fall color. Its prolific seed production can be a problem, however.

OTHER COMMON NAMES: Mexican fireweed, belvedere, burning bush.

DESCRIPTION: Summer cypress has narrow, pointed, hairy leaves that are 1–2 inches (2.5–5 cm) long, with no leaf stem. The leaves alternate along the upright, many-branched stem and turn bright red in fall. Small, green, petal-less flowers bloom in the leaf axils (where the leaves join the stem) from midsummer through early fall. The seeds are enclosed in a star-shaped covering. Plants grow from a taproot.

HEIGHT: Summer cypress can grow from 3 inches (7.5 cm) to 6 feet (1.8 m) tall or more.

PREFERRED SITE AND CLIMATE: This weed grows in dry farm fields, pastures, and unmowed areas in the northern half of the United States, except in Washington, western Idaho, and western Montana.

LIFE CYCLE: Annual.

HOW IT SPREADS: By seed.

SUGGESTED CONTROLS: Mulch to prevent existing seeds from sprouting. Hoe, pull, or flame seedlings as soon as you spot them. Pull, dig, cut, or mow larger plants before they set seed. If you don't dig or pull out the taproot, keep cutting or mowing every week or two until plants stop resprouting.

PRICKLY LETTUCE

HENBIT

Prickly lettuce has dandelion-like yellow flowers in summer and fall, followed by black seeds. The seeds have a tuft of hair at the end and are carried by the wind.

A member of the mint family, henbit spreads by seed and by square stems that root as they creep over the soil. It grows most vigorously in cool, damp weather.

DESCRIPTION: Prickly lettuce looks much like a tall dandelion plant. Its upright stem is prickly at the base, and it oozes a milky sap when broken. The leaves are lobed like dandelion leaves and have a row of short prickles along the midvein on the underside. The small flower heads have yellow ray flowers (petals) like dandelion blooms. Prickly lettuce flowers are about ¼ inch (6 mm) wide and bloom at the top of the plant in midsummer through early fall. Plants grow from a large, deep taproot.

HEIGHT: This plant can reach 2–6 feet (60–180 cm) tall.

PREFERRED SITE AND CLIMATE: Prickly lettuce grows in dry soil along roadsides and in orchards, fencerows, and unmowed areas throughout the United States, except in northern Maine and southern Florida.

LIFE CYCLE: Annual, winter annual, or biennial.

HOW IT SPREADS: By seed.

SUGGESTED CONTROLS: Mulch to prevent existing seeds from sprouting. Hoe, pull, or flame seedlings as soon as you spot them. Pull, dig, cut, or mow larger plants before they set seed. If you don't dig or pull out the taproot, keep cutting or mowing every week or two until plants stop resprouting.

DESCRIPTION: Henbit has an upright, thin, supple, four-sided stem and round leaves with deep scallops on the margin. The upper leaves attach in pairs directly to the stem, while the lower leaves have a leaf stem. In spring and fall, small, pink or blue-purple flowers with two lips and a long neck bloom in whorls above the leaves near the top of the plant.

HEIGHT: Plants grow 4–16 inches (10–40 cm) tall.

PREFERRED SITE AND CLIMATE: Henbit makes a home in rich soil in gardens, lawns, and unmowed areas throughout most of the United States, except in the Dakotas, Montana, and part of Utah.

LIFE CYCLE: Winter annual or biennial.

HOW IT SPREADS: By seed and by stems that root at the nodes (stem joints).

SUGGESTED CONTROLS: Mulch to prevent existing seeds from sprouting. Hoe, pull, or flame seedlings as soon as you spot them. Pull or dig larger plants before they set seed. Let the plants dry in the sun before composting them. Avoid leaving pulled or dug plants on the soil surface in the garden; they may quickly reroot.

COMMENTS: Henbit resembles ground ivy (*Glechoma hederacea*), described on page 117, but is more upright.

Lepidium virginicum   Cruciferae

VIRGINIA PEPPERWEED

Virginia pepperweed is easy to identify by its many tiny, flat seedpods. This annual weed pops up in unmowed areas throughout most of the United States.

OTHER COMMON NAMES: Pepper grass, bird pepper, poor man's pepper.

DESCRIPTION: The upright, many-branched stem of Virginia pepperweed sometimes has very fine hairs. The short, narrow stem leaves have wide teeth on the margin and usually lack a leaf stem. The leaves at the base are larger, wider, and toothed. Small, white, four-petaled flowers are produced through spring. After bloom, the branches are covered with round, flat seedpods that are ⅛ inch (3 mm) wide and have a notch at one end.

HEIGHT: Plants grow 6–18 inches (15–45 cm) tall.

PREFERRED SITE AND CLIMATE: Virginia pepperweed pops up along roadsides and in unmowed areas with dry soil throughout the United States, except in southwestern New Mexico, southern Arizona, and the western Dakotas.

LIFE CYCLE: Annual or winter annual.

HOW IT SPREADS: By seed.

SUGGESTED CONTROLS: Mulch to prevent existing seeds from sprouting. Hoe, pull, or flame seedlings as soon as you spot them. Pull, cut, or mow larger plants before they set seed.

OTHER SPECIES:
   L. campestre, field pepperweed, is similar but has larger seedpods, a hairy stem, and hairy, arrow-shaped leaves. It is an annual or biennial.

Linaria vulgaris   Scrophulariaceae

YELLOW TOADFLAX

Yellow toadflax has pretty blooms and is sometimes grown in flower gardens. If you plant it, set it in a pot or surround it with a barrier strip to restrict its spread.

OTHER COMMON NAMES: Butter-and-eggs, wild snapdragon.

DESCRIPTION: The upright, pale green, leafy stem of yellow toadflax has narrow, pale green leaves and few branches. Flowers bloom in clusters at the top of the plant in late spring through midfall. The flowers are yellow with an orange center, about 1 inch (2.5 cm) long, and look like snapdragon flowers, with two large lips and a spur. Yellow toadflax tends to grow in patches.

HEIGHT: Plants reach 1–2 feet (30–60 cm) tall.

PREFERRED SITE AND CLIMATE: Yellow toadflax grows in unmowed areas and pastures and along roadsides throughout the United States. It is often a problem in orchards.

LIFE CYCLE: Perennial.

HOW IT SPREADS: By seed and rhizomes (creeping underground stems).

SUGGESTED CONTROLS: Pull, hoe, mow, or cut seedlings as soon as you spot them. Dig older plants to get the creeping roots (let the roots dry out thoroughly before you compost them), or cut the stems to the ground. If you hoe, mow, or cut the plants, you'll need to do it again every 1–2 weeks until the roots stop resprouting. Or cover the roots with a dense mulch, such as newspaper, cardboard, or plastic.

| *Lonicera* spp. | Caprifoliaceae | *Lonicera maackii* | Caprifoliaceae |

VINING HONEYSUCKLES

AMUR HONEYSUCKLE

Honeysuckle is sometimes sold as a groundcover or a flowering landscape vine. Some types, however, spread too aggressively for home landscapes.

The whitish to yellowish flowers of amur honeysuckle are followed by red berries. The berries may stay on the plants well into winter if birds can find other food.

DESCRIPTION: Vining honeysuckles are vigorous, deciduous or semi-evergreen climbers. The stems form a trailing mound or climb trees and structures. The oval or sometimes lobed leaves form in pairs along the stem; they are about 3 inches (7.5 cm) long and half as wide. The spring through midsummer flowers have a tube at the base, topped with two unevenly divided lips. Japanese honeysuckle (*Lonicera japonica*) is a particularly pesky species, with fragrant, white to yellow flowers followed by black berries borne singly or in clusters.

HEIGHT: Vines grow to 30 feet (9 m) tall or long.

PREFERRED SITE AND CLIMATE: These vines grow in gardens, orchards, fencerows, and thickets and along the edges of woods in the eastern half of the United States as far north as Michigan.

LIFE CYCLE: Perennial.

HOW IT SPREADS: By seed and by stems that root where they touch the ground.

SUGGESTED CONTROLS: Pull, hoe, mow, or cut seedlings as soon as you spot them. Dig out older plants with a pickax to get the roots, or cut the stems to the ground. If you hoe, mow, or cut the plants, do it again every 1–2 weeks until the roots stop resprouting. Or cover the roots with a dense mulch, such as cardboard, plastic, or landscape fabric, for at least one growing season. Goats can be useful for controlling Japanese honeysuckle in low-maintenance areas.

DESCRIPTION: This large, upright shrub is usually wider than it is tall. The stems are hollow and fuzzy (although they may lose their fuzz as they age). The leaves are dark green on top and pale green beneath, with hairs on the veins and leaf stems; they form in pairs along the main stems. Each leaf grows to 3 inches (7.5 cm) long and is elliptical, with a tapered, pointed end and a wedge-shaped base. Fragrant, broad-lipped flowers bloom in pairs at the end of the stems in late spring and change from whitish to yellowish as they mature. Red berries grow close to the stem; they turn from dull to bright red when ripe.

HEIGHT: Mature plants can reach 15 feet (4.5 m) tall.

PREFERRED SITE AND CLIMATE: Amur honeysuckle adapts to a range of soil conditions and can tolerate considerable shade. It grows in yards, gardens, and fencerows throughout the United States.

LIFE CYCLE: Perennial.

HOW IT SPREADS: By seed and rooting stems.

SUGGESTED CONTROLS: Pull, hoe, mow, or cut seedlings as soon as you spot them. Dig out older plants with a pickax, or cut the stems to the ground. If you hoe, mow, or cut the plants, do it again every 1–2 weeks until the roots stop resprouting. Or cover the roots with a dense mulch, such as cardboard, plastic, or landscape fabric, for at least one growing season.

| *Lysimachia nummularia* | Primulaceae | *Lythrum salicaria* | Lythraceae |

MONEYWORT

PURPLE LOOSESTRIFE

Moneywort is a creeping perennial weed that is occasionally used as a lawn substitute in moist, shady spots where lawn grasses won't grow well.

Purple loosestrife is often grown as a garden perennial. However, several states have outlawed the sale and/or garden use of this plant because of its invasive tendencies.

OTHER COMMON NAMES: Creeping Jenny.

DESCRIPTION: Moneywort is a low-growing, trailing vine with round, shiny, coin-like leaves in pairs along the stem. Yellow, five-petaled flowers bloom on slender stems from mid- to late-summer. The fruit is a rounded capsule containing many seeds.

HEIGHT: The stems cling closely to the soil surface and rarely grow more than 1 inch (2.5 cm) tall.

PREFERRED SITE AND CLIMATE: Moneywort shows up in moist lawns and neglected areas throughout the northeastern and northcentral United States.

LIFE CYCLE: Perennial.

HOW IT SPREADS: By seed and rooting stems.

SUGGESTED CONTROLS: Pull or cut back plants often. For heavy infestations (where the lawn has been choked out), rake vigorously to loosen the stems, then cut or mow the plants close to the ground. Follow this treatment by covering the area with a dense mulch, such as cardboard, newspaper, or plastic, for one growing season.

COMMENTS: This low-growing plant is sometimes used as a lawn substitute in moist, shady spots where grass won't grow. The cultivar 'Aurea' has yellow leaves and is attractive in flower beds and container gardens.

OTHER COMMON NAMES: Spiked loosestrife.

DESCRIPTION: Purple loosestrife has an upright, slightly hairy stem. Slightly fuzzy leaves in pairs or trios are wide at the base but narrower and tapered near the tip; they have no leaf stem. The six-petaled, purplish pink flowers form slender spikes that are wider at the base than at the top. Plants flower all summer.

HEIGHT: Purple loosestrife grows 2–4 feet (60–120 cm) tall.

PREFERRED SITE AND CLIMATE: This noxious weed adapts to a range of soil conditions, but it is especially troublesome in swampy, unmowed areas in the northeastern and northcentral United States.

LIFE CYCLE: Perennial.

HOW IT SPREADS: By seed.

SUGGESTED CONTROLS: Dig plants to get the roots, or cut the stems to the ground. If you hoe, mow, or cut the plants, do it again every 1–2 weeks until the roots stop resprouting. Or cover the roots with a dense mulch, such as newspaper, cardboard, or plastic, for at least one growing season. If possible, improve drainage to discourage plants from returning.

COMMENTS: Purple loosestrife crowds out many less aggressive, native wetland plants that are critical for wildlife. The seeds float and are carried by any moving water.

COMMON MALLOW

PINEAPPLE WEED

Common mallow flowers mature into flat, round seedpods that split into sections like slices of pie. Pull or hoe plants before bloom to prevent reseeding.

Pineapple weed has unusual yellow-green summer and fall flowers over mounds of ferny, fragrant leaves. Its flowers resemble those of chamomile but lack the white petals.

DESCRIPTION: The stems of common mallow either grow upright or lie on the ground with the ends turned upward. The hairy, wide, round, toothed leaves are sometimes slightly lobed, with long, slender leaf stems. Small, white or pale purple, five-petaled flowers bloom singly or in clusters in the leaf axils (where the leaves join the stem) from spring through fall. The round, flat seedpods split into sections like slices of a pie. Plants grow from a short taproot.

HEIGHT: Common mallow usually reaches 4–12 inches (10–30 cm) tall.

PREFERRED SITE AND CLIMATE: Common mallow adapts to a wide range of soil conditions in gardens, lawns, roadsides, and unmowed areas throughout the United States.

LIFE CYCLE: Annual or biennial.

HOW IT SPREADS: By seed.

SUGGESTED CONTROLS: Mulch to prevent existing seeds from sprouting. Hoe, pull, or flame seedlings as soon as you spot them. Pull, cut, or mow larger plants before they set seed.

COMMENTS: Can be confused with ground ivy (*Glechoma hederacea*), described on page 117, but ground ivy has a square stem.

DESCRIPTION: This lacy weed has fern-like, finely divided leaves that smell like pineapple when crushed. The leaves alternate along the upright, branched stem. Yellowish green, cone-shaped flowers bloom at the ends of the branches from summer through early fall.

HEIGHT: Plants grow 6–18 inches (15–45 cm) tall.

PREFERRED SITE AND CLIMATE: You may find pineapple weed in compacted soil in gardens and unmowed areas and along roadsides in the eastern United States and along the Pacific coast.

LIFE CYCLE: Annual.

HOW IT SPREADS: By seed.

SUGGESTED CONTROLS: Mulch to prevent existing seeds from sprouting. Hoe, pull, or flame seedlings as soon as you spot them. Pull, cut, or mow larger plants before they set seed.

COMMENTS: The leaves resemble those of mayweed (*Anthemis cotula*), described on page 91, but have a pleasant pineapple smell.

Black medic

Black medic is a common weed in lawns and meadows throughout the United States. Because it is a legume (like alfalfa and clover), it adds nitrogen to the soil.

OTHER COMMON NAMES: Hop clover, yellow trefoil, none-such.

DESCRIPTION: Black medic has a flexible, branched, sprawling stem. Its clover-like leaves consist of three leaflets; the center leaflet has a leaf stem, but the side leaflets do not. The yellow flower head is cone-shaped or round. The black seedpods contain one seed. Plants grow from a shallow taproot.

HEIGHT: Black medic can reach 1–2 feet (30–60 cm) tall in unmowed areas.

PREFERRED SITE AND CLIMATE: This weed grows in lawns, meadows, and unmowed areas and along roadsides throughout the United States.

LIFE CYCLE: Annual, biennial, or perennial.

HOW IT SPREADS: By seed.

SUGGESTED CONTROLS: Mulch to prevent existing seeds from sprouting. Hoe, pull, or flame seedlings as soon as you spot them. Pull, cut, or mow larger plants before they set seed. Fertilize the area with nitrogen to discourage this weed from returning.

Carpetweed

Carpetweed quickly covers bare soil in summer gardens and lawns. Pulling, cutting, or mowing plants before they set seed will keep them from returning next year.

DESCRIPTION: The flexible stem of carpetweed branches at the base. The plant sprawls on the ground in all directions to form a mat. Clusters of five or six narrow leaves form whorls around the stem at the nodes (stem joints). Several small, white flowers form at the leaf axils (where the leaves join the stem) in mid- to late-summer. The taproot branches only slightly.

HEIGHT: Plants grow 2–12 inches (5–30 cm) tall.

PREFERRED SITE AND CLIMATE: Carpetweed tolerates a wide range of soil conditions in gardens, lawns, and unmowed areas throughout the United States, except in North Dakota and Montana.

LIFE CYCLE: Annual.

HOW IT SPREADS: By seed.

SUGGESTED CONTROLS: Mulch to prevent existing seeds from sprouting. Hoe, pull, or flame seedlings as soon as you spot them. Pull, cut, or mow larger plants before they set seed.

COMMENTS: Carpetweed starts growing in the summer and grows quickly, especially over fertile, bare soil. It can be confused with catchweed bedstraw (*Galium aparine*), described on page 115, but catchweed bedstraw is sticky and hairy.

NIMBLEWILL

Nimblewill is a real pest in lawns. This perennial weed produces stolons that run along the soil surface and root at the joints to form a spreading patch.

DESCRIPTION: Nimblewill has wiry, thin, spreading stems. Flat leaves are ½–2 inches (12–50 mm) long and perpendicular to the stem. The collar, where the blade meets the stem, may have a few hairs. In the fall, nimblewill bears feathery, slender flower heads that are 2–6 inches (5–15 cm) long.

HEIGHT: Plants can grow 6–24 inches (15–60 cm) tall; in lawns, they adapt to whatever mowing height you use.

PREFERRED SITE AND CLIMATE: Nimblewill makes a home in damp lawns, fencerows, and unmowed areas in the eastern half of the United States.

LIFE CYCLE: Perennial.

HOW IT SPREADS: By seed and stolons.

SUGGESTED CONTROLS: Dig plants to get the creeping stems (let them dry out thoroughly in the sun before you compost them), or cut the stems to the ground. If you hoe, mow, or cut the plants, you'll need to do it again every 1–2 weeks until the roots stop resprouting. Or cover the roots with a dense mulch, such as newspaper, cardboard, or plastic, for one growing season. If possible, improve drainage to discourage plants from returning.

COMMENTS: Nimblewill resembles bermuda grass (*Cynodon dactylon*), described on page 106, and marsh bent grass (*Agrostis palustris*), described on page 87.

YELLOW WOODSORREL

Yellow woodsorrel is a widespread lawn and garden weed. Digging plants is probably the best control. If you leave the root in the ground, it will just keep resprouting.

DESCRIPTION: Yellow woodsorrel is a low, bushy lawn weed. Its leaves resemble those of clover, with three heart-shaped leaflets. Small, yellow, five-petaled flowers form clusters; they bloom from late spring through midfall. Plants grow from a taproot.

HEIGHT: Yellow woodsorrel normally reaches 4–18 inches (10–45 cm) tall.

PREFERRED SITE AND CLIMATE: This pesky weed pops up in dry lawns, pathways, neglected areas, and bare soil throughout the United States.

LIFE CYCLE: Perennial.

HOW IT SPREADS: By seed.

SUGGESTED CONTROLS: Pull, hoe, mow, or cut seedlings as soon as you spot them. Dig out older plants or cut the stems to the ground. If you hoe, mow, or cut the plants, do it again every 1–2 weeks until the roots stop resprouting. Or cover the roots with a dense mulch, such as newspaper, cardboard, or plastic, for at least one growing season. For infestations in lawns, remove as much of the weed as you can by hand, and fertilize the lawn to help the grass crowd out the weeds.

COMMENTS: Although yellow woodsorrel resembles clover, the two plants are not related.

| *Panicum capillare* | Gramineae | | *Paspalum dilatatum* | Gramineae |

WITCH GRASS

DALLIS GRASS

Witch grass is an annual weed that pops up throughout much of the United States. Cutting the plants down before they set seed will reduce problems with this weed.

Sometimes grown as a pasture grass for grazing animals, dallis grass is a weed when it appears in your lawn. It spreads by seed and rhizomes (creeping underground stems).

DESCRIPTION: This hairy grass has upright stems that are usually spreading and branched at the base. The flower head is a loose, open cluster (panicle) that resembles a broom. The flower head makes up about half of the plant's height. A fringe of hairs grows at the collar, where the blade meets the stem.

HEIGHT: This grassy weed usually grows 10–30 inches (25–75 cm) tall; in lawns, it can adapt to whatever mowing height you use.

PREFERRED SITE AND CLIMATE: Witch grass tolerates a wide range of soil conditions in lawns, gardens, meadows, and unmowed areas throughout the United States, except in the most northern Plains states.

LIFE CYCLE: Annual.

HOW IT SPREADS: By seed.

SUGGESTED CONTROLS: Mulch to prevent existing seeds from sprouting. Hoe, pull, or flame seedlings as soon as you spot them. Pull, cut, or mow larger plants before they set seed.

OTHER SPECIES:
   P. dichotomiflorum, fall panicum, can grow 20–50 inches (50–130 cm) tall. It is hairless or only slightly hairy, with a flower head that is sparser, more compact, and shorter. The stems may have a purple tinge. The leaf blade has a prominent white vein down the middle. Fall panicum often grows in low areas.

DESCRIPTION: Dallis grass has yellow-green leaf blades that are about ½ inch (12 mm) wide, with rough edges and a white vein down the middle. The blades may have sparse hairs at their bases. A tall, rounded membrane forms where the inner surface of the blade meets the stem. The seed head consists of a stem with three to six spikelets at about a 45 degree angle to the stem. Dallis grass grows in spreading clumps.

HEIGHT: Plants can reach 18–72 inches (45–180 cm) tall; they are shorter in mowed areas.

PREFERRED SITE AND CLIMATE: Dallis grass grows in lawns and marshes in the southern half of the eastern United States, along parts of the Pacific coast, and in southern California, Arizona, and New Mexico.

LIFE CYCLE: Perennial.

HOW IT SPREADS: By seed and short rhizomes.

SUGGESTED CONTROLS: Dig plants to get the creeping stems (let them dry out thoroughly in the sun before you compost them), or cut the stems to the ground. If you hoe, mow, or cut the plants, you'll need to do it again every 1–2 weeks until the roots stop resprouting. Or cover the roots with a dense mulch, such as newspaper, cardboard, or plastic, for one growing season. To discourage the weed from returning, fertilize the lawn to make the grass more vigorous and competitive.

| *Phalaris arundinacea* Gramineae | *Phragmites australis* Gramineae |

REED CANARY GRASS

COMMON REED

Reed canary grass normally grows in large patches. It is useful for preventing erosion in ditches and other wet areas, but it usually isn't welcome in a home landscape.

Common reed is a pernicious perennial grass that takes over wet-soil areas and crowds out other vegetation. It is difficult to control and demands persistent efforts.

DESCRIPTION: This coarse grass has flat leaf blades that are 3–8 inches (7.5–20 cm) long and ½ inch (12 mm) or more wide. The blades have pointed tips and rough edges. A tall membrane that has hairs on the back forms where the inner surface of the blade meets the stem; this membrane may sometimes be torn. The seed head is a dense, spike-like panicle that's 2–8 inches (5–20 cm) long. Plants usually grow in large patches.

HEIGHT: Stems reach 2–8 feet (60–240 cm) tall.

PREFERRED SITE AND CLIMATE: Reed canary grass grows in wet soil in the northern two-thirds of the United States.

LIFE CYCLE: Perennial.

HOW IT SPREADS: By seed and rhizomes (creeping underground stems).

SUGGESTED CONTROLS: Dig plants to get the creeping roots (let the roots dry out thoroughly before you compost them), or cut the stems to the ground. If you hoe, mow, or cut the plants, you'll need to do it again every 1–2 weeks until the roots stop resprouting. Or cover the roots with a dense mulch, such as newspaper, cardboard, plastic, or landscape fabric, for one growing season. If possible, improve drainage to discourage plants from returning.

COMMENTS: Reed canary grass is useful for preventing erosion in ditches and other wet areas.

OTHER COMMON NAMES: Giant reed.

DESCRIPTION: This huge wetland grass has upright stems. The broad, flat leaf blades are 6–24 inches (15–60 cm) long and ⅓–2 inches (1–5 cm) wide. Plants bear large, dense, purplish flower panicles from midsummer through early fall.

HEIGHT: Common reed may grow 7–21 feet (2–6 m) tall.

PREFERRED SITE AND CLIMATE: This spreading grass grows in wetlands throughout the United States, except in the inland areas of the southern states along the Atlantic coast and in the south central states.

LIFE CYCLE: Perennial.

HOW IT SPREADS: By seed, rhizomes (creeping underground stems), and sometimes stolons (creeping aboveground stems).

SUGGESTED CONTROLS: Dig plants to get the creeping roots (let the roots dry out thoroughly in the sun before you compost them), or cut the stems to the ground. If you hoe, mow, or cut the plants, do it again every 1–2 weeks until the roots stop resprouting. Or cover the roots with a dense mulch, such as cardboard, heavy plastic, landscape fabric, or old carpeting, for at least one growing season.

COMMENTS: The stems are sometimes used for weaving mats, nets, and screens.

| *Physalis* spp. | Solanaceae | *Phytolacca americana* | Phytolaccaeae |

GROUND CHERRIES

COMMON POKEWEED

The flowers of ground cherries are yellowish with a brown or purple center. The berry-like fruit is enclosed in a papery sack called a calyx.

The young shoots and small leaves of pokeweed are edible when thoroughly cooked in several changes of water. The berrries, uncooked stems and leaves, and roots are poisonous, however.

DESCRIPTION: Clammy ground cherry (*Physalis heterophylla*) has a hairy stem that branches as the plant matures to form a dense bush. Hairy, oval leaves have pointed tips and scalloped edges. The five-lobed flower is about ¾ inch (18 mm) wide and blooms all summer. Smooth ground cherry (*P. subglabrata*) has an upright, branching stem that is hairy when the plant is young but later becomes smooth. Triangular, smooth or slightly hairy leaves have smooth or slightly toothed edges.

HEIGHT: Both species grow 1–3 feet (30–90 cm) tall.

PREFERRED SITE AND CLIMATE: Clammy ground cherry is found in sandy and gravelly soil in gardens, woods, and unmowed areas in the eastern three-quarters of the United States and in central Washington state. Smooth ground cherry grows in gardens and neglected areas in the northern United States, except in the most northern states.

LIFE CYCLE: Perennial.

HOW IT SPREADS: By seed and rhizomes (creeping underground stems).

SUGGESTED CONTROLS: Dig plants to get the roots (let the roots dry out thoroughly before you compost them), or cut the stems to the ground. If you hoe, mow, or cut the plants, do it again every 1–2 weeks until the roots stop resprouting. Or cover the roots with a dense mulch, such as cardboard or plastic, for one growing season.

DESCRIPTION: The stout, upright, reddish stem of common pokeweed arises from a large, very poisonous taproot. The stem is branched near the top and dies back to the ground each winter. The leaves alternate along the stem and get smaller toward the top of the plant. Small, white flowers are widely spaced along each stem tip from midsummer through early fall. The flowers are followed by narrow, usually drooping clusters of dark purple berries that have red juice.

HEIGHT: Stems can grow 3–9 feet (90–270 cm) tall.

PREFERRED SITE AND CLIMATE: Common pokeweed thrives in rich, deep, gravelly soil in gardens and fields and along roadsides and fencerows.

LIFE CYCLE: Perennial.

HOW IT SPREADS: By seed.

SUGGESTED CONTROLS: Pull or cut seedlings as soon as you spot them. Pull or dig out older plants (getting as much of the root as possible) before they set seed, or hoe, mow, or cut them to the ground every week or two until they stop resprouting. Or cut them back, then cover the area with a dense mulch, such as newspaper, cardboard, or plastic, for one growing season. Common pokeweed does not survive in soil that is dug or tilled periodically, such as in a vegetable garden.

Plantago major   Plantaginaceae

BROAD-LEAVED PLANTAIN

Broad-leaved plantain often grows in heavy, compacted soil. To discourage broad-leaved plantain from returning, aerate the site and add organic matter to loosen the soil.

OTHER COMMON NAMES: Common plantain.

DESCRIPTION: The roundish, waxy leaves of broad-leaved plantain are 3–4 inches (7.5–8 cm) long and form a rosette; they have deep, parallel veins from the tip to the base. The leaf stem cups inward like a trough. Small green flowers bloom on wiry stems from the center of the rosette from early summer through midfall. Each barrel-shaped seedpod has a seam around the middle.

HEIGHT: Plants are 6–18 inches (15–45 cm) tall, although they can be quite flat in areas that are frequently mowed or walked on.

PREFERRED SITE AND CLIMATE: Broad-leaved plantain grows in lawns, pathways, and unmowed areas, especially where the soil is damp, heavy, fertile, and shaded. It is found throughout the United States.

LIFE CYCLE: Perennial.

HOW IT SPREADS: By seed.

SUGGESTED CONTROLS: Cut plants off at the soil surface; repeat every week or two until the root stops resprouting. Or dig or pull the plants, getting as much of the taproot as possible, before they set seed.

OTHER SPECIES:

    P. lanceolata, buckhorn plantain, has leaves that are long, narrow, and hairy.

Poa annua   Gramineae

ANNUAL BLUEGRASS

A cousin of Kentucky bluegrass, annual bluegrass blooms earlier and is paler. It prefers cool weather and adequate moisture; it usually dies in hot weather.

DESCRIPTION: Annual bluegrass grows in shallow-rooted tufts. The lower portion of the stem may lie along the ground and send out roots, while the ends of the stems turn upright. The fine-textured, light green leaf blades are about ⅛ inch (4 mm) wide, with slightly pointed tips. Loose, open, small flower clusters (panicles) bloom throughout the growing season.

HEIGHT: Plants can grow to 12 inches (30 cm) tall; in lawns, the height depends on the mowing height you use.

PREFERRED SITE AND CLIMATE: Annual bluegrass grows in lawns and gardens throughout the United States.

LIFE CYCLE: Annual.

HOW IT SPREADS: By seed.

SUGGESTED CONTROLS: In gardens, mulch to prevent existing seeds from sprouting. Pull or hoe plants as soon as you spot them to prevent them from setting seed. In lawns, pull out what you can or just tolerate it. Fertilizing the lawn may promote the growth of desirable perennial grasses that can crowd out this annual. Overseeding with perennial grasses can also help. To control large infestations, consider solarizing the area and starting a new lawn from scratch.

PROSTRATE KNOTWEED

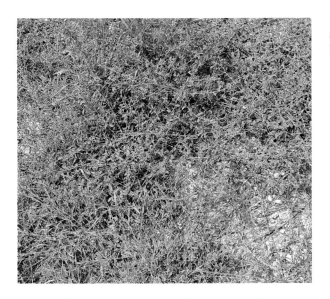

Prostrate knotweed is a common sight in lawns and pathways where the soil is hard and compacted. The small flowers bloom from summer into fall and produce many seeds.

DESCRIPTION: The wiry stems of prostrate knotweed usually lie flat on the soil surface, forming a mat, although they sometimes grow upward. The small, blue-green leaves vary in shape but generally are oblong, with a pointed tip. The nodes (stem joints) have a papery covering. Small white or yellow flowers bloom at the axils (where the leaves join the stem) from midsummer through late fall.

HEIGHT: Plants usually grow 6–24 inches (15–60 cm) tall.

PREFERRED SITE AND CLIMATE: Prostrate knotweed shows up in lawns, disturbed soil, and waste areas and along roadsides throughout the United States, especially where the soil is hard and compacted.

LIFE CYCLE: Annual.

HOW IT SPREADS: By seed.

SUGGESTED CONTROLS: Mulch to prevent existing seeds from sprouting. Hoe, pull, or flame seedlings as soon as you spot them. Pull, cut, or mow larger plants before they set seed. Aerate the soil to discourage this weed from coming back.

COMMENTS: Can be confused with spotted spurge (*Euphorbia maculata*), described on page 114.

OTHER SPECIES:

P. erectum, erect knotweed, resembles prostrate knotweed but is upright and has paler leaves and stems.

WILD BUCKWHEAT

The twining stems of wild buckwheat wrap around other plants for support. This weed is difficult to eliminate; controlling plants before they set seed is critical.

DESCRIPTION: This creeping, twining vine branches at the base. The nodes (stem joints) have a papery covering. Heart-shaped, pointed leaves alternate along the stem. Small, greenish white flowers bloom in the leaf axils (where the leaves join the stem) from late spring through late fall.

HEIGHT: Plants grow 8–38 inches (20–95 cm) tall.

PREFERRED SITE AND CLIMATE: Wild buckwheat sprouts up in gardens, thickets, fencerows, and unmowed areas throughout the United States.

LIFE CYCLE: Annual.

HOW IT SPREADS: By seed.

SUGGESTED CONTROLS: Mulch to prevent existing seeds from sprouting. Hoe, pull, or flame seedlings as soon as you spot them. Pull, cut, or mow larger plants before they set seed.

COMMENTS: Wild buckwheat can be confused with field bindweed (*Convolvulus arvensis*), described on page 104; to distinguish them, look for wild buckwheat's papery covering at the nodes.

LADY'S-THUMB

COMMON PURSLANE

Lady's-thumb is a pesky annual weed that spreads by shiny black seeds. Pull out, cut down, or mow plants as soon as you notice them to prevent them from producing seed.

DESCRIPTION: The smooth or slightly hairy, upright, branching stem of lady's-thumb is swollen at the nodes (stem joints). A papery sheath covers each node; the top of the sheath has a fringe of bristles. Leaves that are 1–6 inches (2.5–15 cm) long and pointed at both ends alternate along the stem and may have a dark splotch in the middle. The flower heads are short pink or purple spikes that bloom from early summer through midfall.

HEIGHT: Lady's-thumb may grow 6–36 inches (15–90 cm) tall.

PREFERRED SITE AND CLIMATE: Look for this weed along roadsides and in unmowed areas, especially moist areas, throughout the eastern United States and in the northern half of the western United States.

LIFE CYCLE: Annual.

HOW IT SPREADS: By seed.

SUGGESTED CONTROLS: Mulch to prevent existing seeds from sprouting. Hoe, pull, or flame seedlings as soon as you spot them. Pull, cut, or mow larger plants before they set seed.

OTHER SPECIES:

　　P. pensylvanicum, Pennsylvania smartweed, is nearly identical, but lacks the bristles on the papery covering at the node and is less likely to have a splotch on the leaf.

Common purslane is a familiar sight in gardens across the United States. In hot areas, the plants may go dormant during summer but will return with cool weather.

OTHER COMMON NAMES: Pusley.

DESCRIPTION: Common purslane is a low-growing weed with red-tinged stems and fleshy, succulent leaves that grow in clusters. The stems grow flat or may turn up at the ends; they form mats that may be 1 foot (30 cm) wide. Small, yellow flowers may bloom in the leaf axils (where the leaves join the stem) from early summer until frost.

HEIGHT: This weed reaches 6–12 inches (15–30 cm) tall.

PREFERRED SITE AND CLIMATE: Common purslane is found in gardens and orchards throughout the United States. It tolerates dry conditions.

LIFE CYCLE: Annual.

HOW IT SPREADS: By seed that germinates in warm soil. It sets seed until frost, stopping only during the hottest part of summer.

SUGGESTED CONTROLS: Mulch to prevent existing seeds from sprouting. Hoe, pull, or flame seedlings as soon as you spot them. Pull, cut, or mow larger plants before they set seed. Because the stems reroot readily, take care to remove all plant pieces from the garden.

COMMENTS: Purslane leaves and stems are edible raw or cooked.

| *Potentilla* spp. | Rosaceae | *Prunella vulgaris* | Labiatae |

CINQUEFOILS

HEAL-ALL

Cinquefoils have rough, hairy stems, usually yellow flowers, and leaves consisting of a circle of leaflets. Most spread by seed; common cinquefoil also has tubers.

You can tell that heal-all is in the mint family by its square stems. The stems are usually upright but will change to a creeping form where they're mowed or walked on.

DESCRIPTION: Rough cinquefoil (*P. norvegica*) may be semi-upright or spreading. The leaves consist of three hairy, toothed leaflets with blunt tips. Small, inconspicuous flowers bloom at the ends of the branches from midsummer through early fall. Common cinquefoil (*P. simplex*) has low-growing stems that root at the nodes. The leaves have five leaflets and toothed margins. The flowers bloom in spring.

HEIGHT: Rough cinquefoil grows 1–3 feet (30–90 cm) tall; common cinquefoil reaches only 4–6 inches (10–15 cm) tall.

PREFERRED SITE AND CLIMATE: Cinquefoils are common along roadsides and in thickets and unmowed areas. They tolerate a wide range of soil conditions and grow throughout the United States, except in the most southern states.

LIFE CYCLE: Rough cinquefoil is annual; common cinquefoil is perennial.

HOW IT SPREADS: By seed.

SUGGESTED CONTROLS: Mulch to prevent existing seeds from sprouting. Hoe, pull, or flame seedlings as soon as you spot them. Pull or dig out older plants (getting as much of the root as possible) before they set seed, or hoe, mow, or cut them to the ground every week or two until they stop resprouting. Or cut them back, then cover the area with a dense mulch, such as newspaper, cardboard, or plastic, for one growing season.

OTHER COMMON NAMES: Self-heal.

DESCRIPTION: The four-sided, upright or spreading stems of heal-all are hairy when the plant is young but become smooth as it matures. The somewhat triangular leaves are 1–4 inches (2.5–10 cm) long, grow in pairs along the stem, and have long leaf stems. The leaves may be hairy and can have smooth or slightly notched edges. Blue or purple, tube-shaped flowers with two lips bloom in spikes at the ends of branches.

HEIGHT: Plants may be anywhere from 2–24 inches (5–60 cm) tall.

PREFERRED SITE AND CLIMATE: Heal-all thrives in moist lawns and unmowed areas throughout the United States, except in most areas of the Dakotas, Utah, and Montana.

LIFE CYCLE: Perennial.

HOW IT SPREADS: By seed and by stolons that root at the nodes.

SUGGESTED CONTROLS: Dig plants to get the creeping stems (let them dry out thoroughly in the sun before you compost them), or cut the stems to the ground. If you hoe, mow, or cut the plants, you'll need to do it again every 1–2 weeks until the roots stop resprouting. Or cover the roots with a dense mulch, such as newspaper, cardboard, or plastic, for one growing season. If possible, improve drainage to discourage plants from returning.

KUDZU

Kudzu is a fast-growing, aggressive vine that can quickly engulf telephone poles, fences, and trees. Controlling large areas of this vine requires persistence!

OTHER COMMON NAMES: Kudzuvine.

DESCRIPTION: Kudzu's sometimes-lobed leaves consist of three leaflets, 3–6 inches (7.5–15 cm) long, with pointed ends and a lopsided base near the leaf stalk (petiole). The leaves alternate along the stem. Small, purple, grape-scented, pea-like flowers grow in clusters from late summer through early fall. The seeds form in small, long, hairy seedpods. The vine grows from large, starchy tubers.

HEIGHT: A single vine may grow to 60 feet (18 m) long or more in one season.

PREFERRED SITE AND CLIMATE: Kudzu adapts to a wide range of soil conditions along roadsides and in woodlands and unmowed areas. It is most common in the southeastern United States but also grows in the middle Atlantic states.

LIFE CYCLE: Perennial.

HOW IT SPREADS: By seed and by trailing stems that root and produce new plants.

SUGGESTED CONTROLS: Digging out the deep-set tubers is difficult, and it's inevitable that you'll miss a few. Pull, hoe, mow, or cut shoots or existing plants to the ground every 1–2 weeks until the plants stop resprouting. Or cut them back, then cover the area with a dense mulch, such as landscape fabric, for at least one growing season (two or three seasons are more effective).

BUTTERCUPS

Tall buttercup contains an acid juice that can irritate the mouth and intestines of animals if they eat it. Improving drainage can discourage this weed from returning.

DESCRIPTION: Tall buttercup (*R. acris*) has an upright, hairy stem that branches near the top. Hairy leaves are divided into narrow, pointed segments like the fingers on a hand. The late-spring through early-fall flowers are usually yellow but may be cream-colored and have five to seven overlapping petals. Creeping buttercup (*R. repens*) has light blotches on the leaves and creeping runners that send up leaves. The midspring through early-summer flowers have five or seven yellow petals.

HEIGHT: Tall buttercup reaches 1–3 feet (30–90 cm) tall, creeping buttercup grows along the ground.

PREFERRED SITE AND CLIMATE: Buttercups thrive in unmowed, moist areas. Tall buttercup grows throughout the United States, except in the Dakotas and eastern Montana. Creeping buttercup grows in the northern half of the United States, except in the Dakotas and eastern Montana.

LIFE CYCLE: Perennial.

HOW IT SPREADS: By seed. Creeping buttercup also has stolons.

SUGGESTED CONTROLS: Mulch to prevent existing seeds from sprouting. Dig plants to get the roots, or cut the stems to the ground. If you hoe, mow, or cut the plants, do it again every 1–2 weeks until the roots stop resprouting. Or cover the roots with a dense mulch, such as newspaper, cardboard, or plastic, for one growing season.

Rhus glabra	Anacardiaceae	*Rosa multiflora*	Rosacea

SMOOTH SUMAC

MULTIFLORA ROSE

Smooth sumac can be attractive in natural plantings. Mowing the young outer shoots as they emerge will keep the plants from spreading if you need to contain them.

Multiflora rose was once widely planted for hedges, and it is often used as the rootstock for grafted garden roses. In most cases, though, it is considered a weed.

DESCRIPTION: Smooth sumac is a suckering shrub that usually grows in colonies. Leaves to 2 feet (60 cm) long alternate along the thick stem that may be smooth and hairless or covered with a fine white fuzz. Each leaf consists of a leaf stalk lined with pairs of leaflets 2–5 inches (5–12.5 cm) long. The leaflets are coated with a fine white fuzz on the back and turn bright red in the fall. Greenish clusters of flowers covered with tiny hairs bloom from late spring through midsummer. The fruit is a cone-shaped, reddish, fuzzy cluster.

HEIGHT: Plants can reach 10–15 feet (3–5 m) tall.

PREFERRED SITE AND CLIMATE: Smooth sumac is found in unmowed areas and along woodland edges throughout much of the United States.

LIFE CYCLE: Perennial.

HOW IT SPREADS: By seed and suckers.

SUGGESTED CONTROLS: Pull, hoe, mow, or cut seedlings as soon as you spot them. Dig older plants to get the roots (let the roots dry out thoroughly before you compost them), or cut the stems to the ground. If you hoe, mow, or cut the plants, do it again every 1–2 weeks until the roots stop re-sprouting, or cover the roots with a dense mulch, such as cardboard or plastic, for one growing season.

OTHER SPECIES:

R. typhina, staghorn sumac, is similar, but the trunk and branches are hairy.

DESCRIPTION: Multiflora rose is a common wild rose with thorny, arching canes. The leaves are usually made up of seven or nine leaflets in pairs along the leaf stem. The leaflets are bright green on top and may be fuzzy on the bottom; they are usually less than 1½ inches (3 cm) long, with a sharp-toothed edge. The leaflet tip can be pointed or blunt and the base is wedge-shaped. White or pinkish, fragrant flowers about ¾ inch (18 mm) wide bloom in early summer.

HEIGHT: Canes may grow to 10 feet (3 m) tall.

PREFERRED SITE AND CLIMATE: Multiflora rose tolerates a wide range of soil conditions. It grows throughout the United States, except in the Rocky Mountains, deserts, and southeastern coastal plains.

LIFE CYCLE: Perennial.

HOW IT SPREADS: By seed and by stems that root at the tip.

SUGGESTED CONTROLS: Pull, mow, or cut seedlings as soon as you spot them. Cut the stems of older plants to the ground with long-handled pruners. (Always wear sturdy gloves when handling the prickly canes!) Dig out the remaining crown and roots with a pickax, or cut down the new shoots every 1–2 weeks until the roots stop resprouting. Or cover the roots with a dense mulch, such as cardboard, plastic, or landscape fabric, for at least one growing season.

BRAMBLES

Wineberries have long, prickly canes covered with reddish hairs. They produce tasty fruit but can be invasive in and along wooded areas.

If you grow brambles, such as blackberries, for their fruit, prune out the old canes each year and dig up unwanted suckers to keep plants under control.

DESCRIPTION: Brambles have many long, usually prickly, tangled stems—called canes—that bend to the ground. Their summer flowers are usually white or pink, and their berries are often edible. Blackberry (*R. macropetalus*), also called dewberry, has canes that grow upward, then droop. The prickles bend when pressed. The leaves consist of three leaflets that have sharp teeth on the edges. The clusters of white flowers are followed by black berries. Black raspberry (*R. occidentalis*), also known as thimbleberry, has canes that grow upright, then bend to the soil and root at the tip. The leaves consist of three leaflets with a toothed edge and a fuzzy white coating on the back. The small white flowers are borne in dense clusters on prickly flower stems and followed by black or amber berries. Wineberry (*R. phoenicolasius*) has long canes that bend over and root at the tip and are covered with soft, straight prickles and reddish hairs. The leaves consist of three broad, heart-shaped leaflets with a toothed edge, purplish veins, and a white coating on the underside. White or pink flowers grow in tight clusters, followed by bright red, edible berries.

HEIGHT: Canes average 3–5 feet (90–150 cm) tall.

PREFERRED SITE AND CLIMATE: Brambles adapt to a wide range of soil conditions in open areas and light shade. They are found throughout the United States.

LIFE CYCLE: Perennial. Individual canes are biennial, fruiting the second year.

HOW IT SPREADS: By seed and rooting canes.

SUGGESTED CONTROLS: Pull, mow, or cut seedlings as soon as you spot them. Cut the stems of older plants to the ground. (Wear sturdy gloves when handling the prickly canes!) Dig out the remaining crown and roots with a pickax, cut down the new shoots every 1–2 weeks until the roots stop resprouting, or cover the roots with a dense mulch, such as cardboard, plastic, or landscape fabric, for at least one growing season.

RED SORREL

Red sorrel tends to grow in patches. It doesn't compete well with other plants, so fertilizing your lawn to encourage the growth of the grass can inhibit this weed.

OTHER COMMON NAMES: Sheep sorrel.

DESCRIPTION: Young red sorrel plants have just a rosette of leaves near the ground. Thin, upright stems that branch near the top emerge as the plant gets older. Several stems may grow from a single crown. The small, arrow-shaped, thick leaves are about 1–3 inches (2.5–7.5 cm) long. Small red or yellow flowers bloom on spikes near the top of the plant.

HEIGHT: Plants grow 6–18 inches (15–45 cm) tall.

PREFERRED SITE AND CLIMATE: Red sorrel is common in bare spots in lawns and neglected areas that are acid, infertile, or poorly drained. It is found throughout the United States.

LIFE CYCLE: Perennial.

HOW IT SPREADS: By seed and rhizomes (creeping underground stems).

SUGGESTED CONTROLS: Pull, hoe, mow, or cut seedlings as soon as you spot them. Dig older plants to get the creeping roots (let the roots dry out thoroughly before you compost them), or cut the stems to the ground. If you hoe, mow, or cut the plants, you'll need to do it again every 1–2 weeks until the roots stop resprouting. Or cover the roots with a dense mulch, such as newspaper, cardboard, or plastic, for one growing season. To discourage the weed from returning, improve soil fertility and drainage. If the soil is acid, apply limestone to raise the pH closer to 7.

CURLY DOCK

Curly dock is a tenacious perennial weed that grows from a large, branched taproot. It's easiest to control this weed as a seedling, before the taproot gets established.

DESCRIPTION: Curly dock produces one or more upright stems that arise from the base of the plant. The wavy- or curly-edged leaves are 6–12 inches (15–30 cm) long. The upper leaves alternate along the stem, and the leaves near the base have a papery covering. The summer flowers form dense clusters at the end of the main stems and turn from green to reddish brown as they mature. The seeds have papery, smooth-edged wings.

HEIGHT: The stems may reach 1–4 feet (30–120 cm) tall.

PREFERRED SITE AND CLIMATE: Curly dock adapts to a wide range of soil conditions in gardens and unmowed areas and along roadsides throughout the United States.

LIFE CYCLE: Perennial.

HOW IT SPREADS: By seed.

SUGGESTED CONTROLS: Mulch to discourage existing weeds from sprouting. Dig plants, or hoe or cut them to the ground every week or two until they stop resprouting. Or cut them down and cover the area with a dense mulch, such as cardboard, newspaper, or plastic, for one growing season.

OTHER SPECIES:

R. obtusifolia, broad-leaved dock, is similar but has broad, flat, heart-shaped leaves. The papery wings attached to the seeds have toothed edges.

Salsola iberica   Chenopodiaceae

RUSSIAN THISTLE

Russian thistle is a troublesome annual weed. This rigid, spiny-looking plant breaks off at the ground to become a rounded tumbleweed when it matures.

DESCRIPTION: The young stems of Russian thistle are soft and green but become stiff and woody as the plant ages. Cylindrical, narrow leaves are long and soft when young and short and stiff with sharp points when older. The small flowers have no petals. They bloom from midsummer until frost on the upper branches in the leaf axils (where the leaves meet the stem). The plant turns red as it matures.

HEIGHT: This weed grows 1–3 feet (30–90 cm) tall.

PREFERRED SITE AND CLIMATE: Russian thistle is most troublesome in dry sites along the Atlantic coast, in the coastal Southeast, and in the western half of the United States.

LIFE CYCLE: Annual.

HOW IT SPREADS: By seed.

SUGGESTED CONTROLS: Mulch to prevent existing seeds from sprouting. Hoe, pull, or flame seedlings as soon as you spot them. Pull, cut, or mow larger plants before they set seed.

COMMENTS: This species is also known as *S. kali* var. *tenuifolia.*

Saponaria officinalis   Caryophyllaceae

BOUNCING BET

The stem and rhizomes of bouncing bet make a soapy solution when crushed in water. They were used in early America as a soap substitute.

DESCRIPTION: Bouncing bet has upright, thick stems that are usually unbranched. The leaves attach in pairs directly to the stem, with no leaf stem, and are 2–3 inches (5–7.5 cm) long. Flowers are about 1 inch (2.5 cm) wide, with five pink or white petals above a long tube. They bloom in clusters at the top of the stem from midsummer through early fall. Plants often grow in patches.

HEIGHT: Bouncing bet grows 1–2 feet (30–60 cm) tall.

PREFERRED SITE AND CLIMATE: This pretty weed is found along roadsides and in unmowed areas throughout the United States.

LIFE CYCLE: Perennial.

HOW IT SPREADS: By seed and rhizomes (creeping underground stems).

SUGGESTED CONTROLS: Dig or pull plants, or mow or cut them to the ground every week or two until they stop resprouting. Or cut them down, then cover the area with a dense mulch, such as newspaper, cardboard, or plastic, for one growing season.

COMMENTS: Bouncing bet was once grown as an ornamental and is still sometimes included in wildflower plantings. It can be confused with corn cockle (*Agrostemma githago*), described on page 87, which has pink-purple flowers, or white campion (*Silene alba*), described on page 143, which has hairy leaves and stems.

| *Scleranthus annuus* | Caryophyllaceae | *Senecio vulgaris* | Compositae |

KNAWEL

COMMON GROUNDSEL

Knawel is a common lawn and garden weed in dry, sandy soil in the eastern United States. Control plants before they set seed to reduce future problems with this weed.

DESCRIPTION: The short, wiry, hairy or smooth stems of knawel can either grow upright or lie on the ground. Thick, pointed, narrow leaves form in pairs on the stem. A membrane covers the base of the leaf. Tiny green flowers bloom in clusters in the leaf axils (where the leaves join the stem) from spring through fall.

HEIGHT: Plants usually grow 1–4 inches (2.5–10 cm) tall.

PREFERRED SITE AND CLIMATE: Knawel pops up in sandy soil in lawns, gardens, and neglected areas in the eastern third of the United States and along the Pacific coast.

LIFE CYCLE: Winter annual.

HOW IT SPREADS: By seed.

SUGGESTED CONTROLS: Mulch to prevent existing seeds from sprouting. Hoe, pull, or flame seedlings as soon as you spot them. Pull, cut, or mow larger plants before they set seed.

Common groundsel adapts to a variety of growing conditions, but it really thrives in moist, rich soil. The ridged, brown seeds are tipped with a tuft of hair.

DESCRIPTION: Common groundsel has an upright, branched stem with lobed and toothed leaves. Tufts of yellow flowers surrounded by black-tipped bracts bloom from late spring through midfall.

HEIGHT: This weed grows 6–16 inches (15–40 cm) tall.

PREFERRED SITE AND CLIMATE: Common groundsel adapts to a wide range of soil conditions in gardens and neglected areas throughout the northern United States.

LIFE CYCLE: Annual.

HOW IT SPREADS: By seed.

SUGGESTED CONTROLS: Mulch to prevent existing seeds from sprouting. Hoe, pull, or flame seedlings as soon as you spot them; they're most common in spring and fall. Pull, cut, or mow larger plants before they set seed.

OTHER SPECIES:

S. viscosus, stinking groundsel, is similar but slightly taller and odorous, with hairy, sticky leaves and stems. It blooms from mid- to late-summer.

Setaria spp.	Gramineae	*Sida spinosa*	Malvaceae

FOXTAILS

PRICKLY SIDA

Foxtails have flower heads that are long, bristly spikes. The stems are normally upright, but they can grow with a more spreading habit when mowed or stepped on frequently.

When pulling or handling prickly sida, wear gloves to protect your hands, or be very careful not to grab the spiny parts of the stem.

DESCRIPTION: Green foxtail (*S. viridis*) has hairless, rough leaf blades. There is a fringe of hairs on the collar where the blade meets the stem. The flower head is 1–3 inches (2.5–7.5 cm) long and bends downward at the tip. The seeds are green and about ¹⁄₁₆ inch (1.5 mm) long. Yellow foxtail (*S. glauca*) is shorter than green foxtail and usually grows in clumps. The leaves have a few long hairs at the base and may spiral. The seeds are larger than green foxtail's and often yellowish.

HEIGHT: Green foxtail grows 1–3 feet (30–90 cm) tall; yellow foxtail may grow 1–2 feet (30–60 cm) tall. All foxtails can grow and flower much shorter in areas where they are mowed or trampled frequently.

PREFERRED SITE AND CLIMATE: Foxtails tolerate a wide range of soil conditions in gardens, along roadsides, and in neglected areas throughout the United States.

LIFE CYCLE: Annual.

HOW IT SPREADS: By seed.

SUGGESTED CONTROLS: Mulch to prevent existing seeds from sprouting. Hoe, pull, or flame seedlings as soon as you spot them. Pull, cut, or mow larger plants to the ground before they set seed; repeat every week or two until plants stop resprouting.

OTHER COMMON NAMES: Teaweed.

DESCRIPTION: The upright, softly hairy stem of prickly sida has wide branches. Two or three short, blunt spines grow where the stem meets the leaves. The oblong leaves have toothed edges and alternate along the branches. The early-summer through midfall flowers have five pale yellow petals and grow singly or in clusters in the axils (where the leaves join the stem). Plants grow from a long, slender, branching taproot.

HEIGHT: This weed usually reaches 8–38 inches (20–95 cm) tall.

PREFERRED SITE AND CLIMATE: Prickly sida tolerates a wide range of soil conditions in gardens and unmowed areas. It grows in the eastern half of the United States, south of the Great Lakes.

LIFE CYCLE: Annual.

HOW IT SPREADS: By seed.

SUGGESTED CONTROLS: Mulch to prevent existing seeds from sprouting. Hoe, pull, or flame seedlings as soon as you spot them. Pull, cut, or mow larger plants to the ground before they set seed; repeat every week or two until plants stop resprouting. (When pulling or handling the plants, wear gloves to protect your hands, or be careful not to grab the spiny parts of the stem.)

WHITE CAMPION

White campion blooms on upright stems from late spring through early fall. The numerous fragrant, white or pink, five-petaled flowers open at night.

OTHER COMMON NAMES: White cockle, evening lychnis.

DESCRIPTION: The upright, thick, branched stem of white campion is densely covered with sticky hairs. Light green, long, narrow, pointed, hairy leaves attach in pairs directly to the stem, with no leaf stem. Each flower has five petals with notches on the edge and is about ⅔ inch (19 mm) wide. Below the petals is a puffy tube with green stripes.

HEIGHT: White campion grows 1–2½ feet (30–75 cm) tall.

PREFERRED SITE AND CLIMATE: This pretty weed flowers along roadsides and in unmowed areas in the northern half of the United States.

LIFE CYCLE: Biennial or short-lived perennial.

HOW IT SPREADS: Mainly by seed; also by spreading roots that send up flowering stems.

SUGGESTED CONTROLS: Dig or pull plants, or mow or cut them to the ground every week or two until they stop resprouting. Or cut them down, then cover the area with a dense mulch, such as newspaper, cardboard, or plastic, for one growing season.

COMMENTS: This species is also known as *Lychnis alba.* It can be confused with corn cockle (*Agrostemma githago*), described on page 87; or bouncing bet (*Saponaria officinalis*), described on page 140.

HORSENETTLE

Horsenettle spreads by seed and rhizomes (creeping underground stems). Its extensive roots can extend 5 feet (1.5 m) or more into the soil.

DESCRIPTION: The upright, hairy, prickly stem of horsenettle can be branched or unbranched. Oblong leaves with wavy or lobed edges alternate along the stem. The leaves have yellow prickles along the veins and leaf stem. White or pale blue flowers are 1 inch (2.5 cm) wide and have five star-like lobes. They bloom in clusters from late spring through early fall. Clusters of juicy, yellow, poisonous berries about ¼ inch (6 mm) wide wrinkle with age.

HEIGHT: Plants can reach 1–3 feet (30–90 cm) tall.

PREFERRED SITE AND CLIMATE: Horsenettle grows in sandy soil in gardens and unmowed areas. It is found in the eastern half of the United States (except Maine) and in California, Oregon, Nevada, Arizona, and southern Idaho.

LIFE CYCLE: Perennial.

HOW IT SPREADS: By seed and rhizomes (creeping underground stems).

SUGGESTED CONTROLS: Pull or dig plants, getting as much of the root system as you can. (Let the roots dry thoroughly in the sun before composting them.) Hoe, mow, or cut shoots to the ground every week or two until they stop resprouting. Or cut them down, then cover the area with a dense mulch, such as newspaper, cardboard, or plastic.

Solanum nigrum   Solanaceae   *Solidago canadensis*   Compositae

BLACK NIGHTSHADE

CANADA GOLDENROD

Black nightshade can host the same pests and diseases that attack other members of the tomato family. Its green to black seeds are poisonous.

DESCRIPTION: The branched stem of black nightshade can be upright or spreading. The leaves are wide at the base and narrow at the tip and have wavy edges. The leaves alternate along the stem and are 1–3 inches (2.5–7.5 cm) long. White, star-shaped flowers are about ¼ inch (6 mm) wide. The flowers have five petal-like lobes and bloom in clusters from late spring through late fall. Green berries turn black as the seeds ripen.

HEIGHT: Plants grow 1–2 feet (30–60 cm) tall.

PREFERRED SITE AND CLIMATE: Black nightshade makes itself at home in gardens and neglected areas, especially in spots with sandy soil. It is found in the eastern half of the United States.

LIFE CYCLE: Annual.

HOW IT SPREADS: By seed.

SUGGESTED CONTROLS: Mulch to prevent existing seeds from sprouting. Hoe, pull, or flame seedlings as soon as you spot them. Pull, cut, or mow larger plants before they set seed; repeat every week or two if plants resprout.

OTHER SPECIES:
S. dulcamara, bitter nightshade, is a woody vine. The stems are 2–10 feet (60–300 cm) long and either lie on the ground or twine around plants and fences. The leaves are 2–5 inches (5–12.5 cm) long, with lobes at the base that make them look arrow-shaped. The berries turn from green to red.

Canada goldenrod grows from creeping stems and is usually found in clumps. It is occasionally included in meadow gardens for its bright yellow, plume-like blooms.

DESCRIPTION: Canada goldenrod has an upright stem that is hairless at the base and fuzzy near the top. The many leaves practically cover the stem and have parallel veins and sharp teeth on the edges. Yellow flower heads with downward-curving branches bloom from midsummer through early fall.

HEIGHT: Plants can reach 1–5 feet (30–150 cm) tall.

PREFERRED SITE AND CLIMATE: Canada goldenrod grows along open roadsides and in unmowed areas, both moist and dry, in the northeastern quarter of the United States.

LIFE CYCLE: Perennial.

HOW IT SPREADS: By seed and rhizomes (creeping underground stems).

SUGGESTED CONTROLS: Hoe, pull, or flame seedlings as soon as you spot them. Dig out older plants before they set seed, getting as much of the root system as you can. (Let the roots dry thoroughly in the sun before composting them.) Cut down or hoe new shoots that appear every week or two until they stop resprouting. Or cut them to the ground, then cover the area with a dense mulch, such as cardboard, newspaper, or plastic, for one growing season.

COMMENTS: Goldenrod, contrary to its reputation, does not cause hay fever; common ragweed (*Ambrosia artemisifolia*), described on page 90, is the real culprit.

SOWTHISTLES

Annual sowthistle blooms with pale yellow flowers in mid- to late-summer. Control plants by hoeing, pulling, cutting, or mowing before they set seed.

Perennial sowthistle is difficult to control since it spreads by both seed and creeping roots. Dig out as much of the root system as you can, or smother it with mulch.

DESCRIPTION: Sowthistles have yellow, dandelion-like flowers and upright stems that ooze a milky sap when broken. Perennial sowthistle (*Sonchus arvensis*) has a powdery covering on the stem. The dandelion-like leaves are 4–8 inches (10–20 cm) long, with irregular lobes and toothed, spiny edges. They alternate along the stem. The base of the leaf curls next to the stem, resembling an ear lobe. The deep yellow flower heads are about 1½ inches (37 mm) wide. In most areas, they bloom from early summer until frost; in warm regions, they may bloom all year. Tufts of hair carry seeds on the wind. Annual sowthistle (*S. oleraceus*) has deeply lobed leaves with prickles on the edges. The tip of the leaves is triangular. The base of the leaves near the top of the plant has pointed projections that clasp the stem. The mid- to late-summer flowers are pale yellow.

HEIGHT: Perennial sowthistle grows 3–7 feet (90–210 cm) tall; annual sowthistle reaches 1–6 feet (30–180 cm) tall.

PREFERRED SITE AND CLIMATE: Both species tolerate a wide range of soil conditions in unmowed areas, woods, and gardens. Perennial sowthistle grows in most of the northern United States; annual sowthistle grows throughout the United States.

LIFE CYCLE: Perennial sowthistle is, as the name says, perennial; annual sowthistle is annual.

HOW IT SPREADS: By seed. Perennial sowthistle also has rhizomes (creeping underground stems).

SUGGESTED CONTROLS: Mulch to prevent existing seeds from sprouting. Hoe, pull, or flame seedlings as soon as you spot them. Pull, cut, or mow larger plants of annual sowthistle before they set seed. Dig out older plants of perennial sowthistle before they set seed, getting as much of the root system as you can. (Let the roots dry thoroughly in the sun before composting them.) Cut down or hoe new shoots that appear every week or two until they stop resprouting. Or cut them to the ground, then cover the area with a dense mulch, such as cardboard, or plastic, for one growing season.

| *Sorghum halepense* | Gramineae | *Spergula arvensis* | Caryophyllaceae |

JOHNSON GRASS

CORN SPURRY

Johnson grass is a troublesome garden weed. If you dig up plants to control them, let the roots dry thoroughly in the sun before tossing them in your compost pile.

Corn spurry is a wispy annual weed with narrow, thread-like leaves and small white flowers. Pull, cut, mow, or hoe plants before they set seed to control their spread.

OTHER COMMON NAMES: Means-grass, Egyptian millet.

DESCRIPTION: Johnson grass resembles a slender corn plant, with an upright, thick stem that may be tinged with purple. The leaf blades are 6–20 inches (15–50 cm) long and ½–1½ inches (12–37 mm) wide, with a white vein down the center. The flower head is a loose, hairy, purple panicle. The roots produce fleshy, scaly rhizomes that may be reddish. Plants are usually found in patches.

HEIGHT: Johnson grass can grow from 18 inches (45 cm) tall to 6 feet (1.8 m) or more.

PREFERRED SITE AND CLIMATE: This troublesome weed grows in most soil types but prefers fertile soil. Originally a southern weed, Johnson grass has been moving steadily northward. It is now found in all but the northern third of the United States.

LIFE CYCLE: Perennial.

HOW IT SPREADS: By seed and rhizomes (creeping underground stems).

SUGGESTED CONTROLS: If possible, pull or dig plants, getting as many of the rhizomes as you can. Hoe, mow, or cut shoots to the ground every week or two until they stop resprouting. Or cut them back and cover the area with a dense mulch, such as newspaper, cardboard, or plastic, for at least one growing season.

OTHER COMMON NAMES: Toadflax.

DESCRIPTION: The slender, branching stem of corn spurry may be slightly hairy. It either grows upright or spreads along the ground and then curves upward. The thread-like leaves are ½–1 inch (12–25 mm) long and clustered into a circle around the stem. The small white flowers have five petals and bloom in clusters at the ends of the branches from early spring through midfall.

HEIGHT: Corn spurry grows 6–18 inches (15–45 cm) tall.

PREFERRED SITE AND CLIMATE: This weed pops up in sandy and gravelly soil in most of the eastern United States, except in a large area bordered by Illinois on the northwest, western Pennsylvania on the northeast, and central Georgia to the south. It is also found along the Pacific coast and in part of Colorado.

LIFE CYCLE: Annual.

HOW IT SPREADS: By seed.

SUGGESTED CONTROLS: Mulch to prevent existing seeds from sprouting. Hoe, pull, or flame seedlings as soon as you spot them. Pull, cut, or mow larger plants before they set seed.

| *Stellaria media* | Caryophyllaceae | *Tanacetum vulgare* | Compositae |

COMMON CHICKWEED

Common chickweed frequently sprouts up in lawns and gardens. It is especially vigorous during the cool weather of fall and spring, when the soil is moist.

OTHER COMMON NAMES: Stitchwort.

DESCRIPTION: The low, spreading, branched stems of common chickweed have rows of tiny hairs. The leaf stem that attaches the leaf to the main stem also has a row of hairs on one side. Short, oval leaves with pointed tips attach in pairs to the stem. The small, white, star-shaped flowers have five deeply notched petals; they bloom from early spring to early winter.

HEIGHT: Plants usually grow 4–12 inches (10–30 cm) tall.

PREFERRED SITE AND CLIMATE: Common chickweed makes itself at home in lawns, gardens, strawberry beds, and orchards throughout the United States.

LIFE CYCLE: Winter annual or annual.

HOW IT SPREADS: By seed and by creeping stems that root at the node.

SUGGESTED CONTROLS: Mulch to prevent existing seeds from sprouting. Hoe, pull, or flame seedlings as soon as you spot them, being especially vigilant from fall through early spring. Pull, cut, or mow larger plants before they set seed.

COMMON TANSY

Tansy is sometimes grown in gardens for its yellow flowers, which attract beneficial insects and are showy in arrangements. The plants are rampant spreaders, though.

OTHER COMMON NAMES: Golden buttons.

DESCRIPTION: Common tansy has an upright, thick stem that may be hairy or hairless and is branched at the top. The fern-like leaves are made up of many pairs of leaflets along the leaf stem; they have a pungent odor. The leaflets have toothed edges and vary in length, being longer in the center of the leaf than at the base and tip. Yellow, rounded flower heads about ½ inch (12 mm) wide form a flat cluster at the top of the plant. They bloom from mid- to late-summer.

HEIGHT: Plants reach 1–4 feet (30–120 cm) tall.

PREFERRED SITE AND CLIMATE: Tansy grows in gardens and unmowed areas and along roadsides in the northcentral and northeastern United States.

LIFE CYCLE: Perennial.

HOW IT SPREADS: By seed and rhizomes (creeping underground stems).

SUGGESTED CONTROLS: If possible, pull or dig plants, getting as many of the rhizomes as you can, before they set seed. (Let the roots dry thoroughly in the sun before composting them.) Hoe, mow, or cut shoots to the ground every week or two until they stop resprouting. Or cut them back and cover the area with a dense mulch such as newspaper, cardboard, or plastic for at least one growing season.

COMMENTS: Tansy flowers attract beneficial insects and are attractive in arrangements.

Taraxacum officinale   Compositae

DANDELION

Dandelion is one of the most widely known weeds in the United States. Digging out as much of the deep taproot as you can is the key to controlling plants effectively.

DESCRIPTION: The leaves of dandelions are 3–10 inches (7.5–25 cm) long and lobed to varying depths. They form a rosette at the base of the plant. Hollow flower stalks arise from the middle of the rosette; they release a milky sap when you break them. The flower heads are 1–2 inches (2.5–5 cm) wide and made up of yellow ray flowers (petals). Plants usually bloom from early summer until frost; they may flower all year in warm climates. Seeds have tufts of hair that allow them to be carried by the wind.

HEIGHT: Dandelion plants can be anywhere from 1–12 inches (2.5–30 cm) tall or more.

PREFERRED SITE AND CLIMATE: This weed is common in lawns, gardens, and neglected areas throughout the United States, except in the southern tips of Florida, Texas, and California and in southwestern Arizona.

LIFE CYCLE: Perennial.

HOW IT SPREADS: By seed.

SUGGESTED CONTROLS: Dig up the entire plant, including as much of the root as you can, as soon as you see it. Any root left in the ground can produce more plants. Check back in a week or two and remove any new sprouts; repeat as necessary. Or cover the area with a dense mulch, such as newspaper, cardboard, or plastic, for one growing season.

COMMENTS: The young leaves are edible raw or cooked.

Thlaspi arvense   Cruciferae

FIELD PENNYCRESS

Field pennycress produces disc-shaped seedpods with wide, papery wings that are notched at the top. These distinctive seedpods are attractive in dried flower arrangements.

DESCRIPTION: Field pennycress has an upright stem that may be branched near the top. The toothed leaves are ½–2 inches (12–50 mm) long and alternate along the stem. The base of the leaf has long, rounded projections that clasp the stem. White flowers with four petals bloom in clusters on long stems from midspring through late summer.

HEIGHT: Plants grow 4–20 inches (10–50 cm) tall.

PREFERRED SITE AND CLIMATE: Field pennycress adapts to a wide range of soil conditions in gardens and unmowed areas and along roadsides throughout the United States.

LIFE CYCLE: Annual or winter annual.

HOW IT SPREADS: By seed.

SUGGESTED CONTROLS: Mulch to prevent existing seeds from sprouting. Hoe, pull, or flame seedlings as soon as you spot them. Pull, cut, or mow larger plants before they set seed.

Toxicodendron radicans   Anacardiaceae

POISON IVY

All parts of the poison ivy plant contain a toxic oil that can cause painful blisters. Wear gloves, long pants, a long-sleeved shirt, and boots when working around this weed.

Poison ivy often grows as a vine, but it will also crawl over the ground if there's nothing for it to climb. It spreads by seed and creeping underground roots.

<u>OTHER COMMON NAMES</u>: Cow-itch, mercury.

<u>DESCRIPTION</u>: Poison ivy grows either as a low shrub or as a vine that climbs trees and fences. As a vine, it sends out clinging roots along the stem. The leaves have three shiny, sometimes hairy leaflets that are 2–4 inches (5–10 cm) long. The leaflets are pointed at the tip, with smooth or toothed margins. The center leaflet has a longer leaf stem than the two side leaflets. The shape of the leaflets is quite variable, sometimes making identification difficult. The leaves turn reddish in the fall. Small, green, five-petaled flowers bloom in clusters in summer. The fruit is a hard, white berry.

<u>HEIGHT</u>: The vines can grow to 150 feet (45 m) long.

<u>PREFERRED SITE AND CLIMATE</u>: Poison ivy adapts to a wide range of soil conditions. It grows in gardens, woods, fencerows, and orchards throughout the United States.

<u>LIFE CYCLE</u>: Perennial.

<u>HOW IT SPREADS</u>: By seed and by underground roots that can spread for many feet before surfacing.

<u>SUGGESTED CONTROLS</u>: Pull, hoe, or cut seedlings as soon as you spot them. If you are not sensitive to the toxic oil in the leaves and stems, you could dig out older plants with a pickax to get the creeping roots. For most people, though, the best approach is to cut the stems to the ground (winter is a good time, since you won't have the leaves to deal with); then cover the roots with a dense mulch, such as cardboard, heavy plastic, old carpeting, or landscape fabric, for at least one growing season. Goats can be useful for controlling poison ivy in low-maintenance areas.

<u>COMMENTS</u>: This species is also known as *Rhus radicans*. All parts of the plant contain a toxic oil that can cause painful blisters, even with light contact. The smoke from burning plants can also cause blistering. Wear gloves (preferably disposable ones), a long-sleeved shirt, long pants, and boots when doing any work around poison ivy. Be aware that the oil can also stay on tools, like clippers and shovels, that are used around the plants. Do not compost the leaves or stems, or you may come in contact with the oil when you handle unfinished compost.

Tragopogon spp. Compositae

SALSIFY

Salsify flowers are open in the morning and tend to close by noon. This plant is sometimes grown in gardens for its edible roots; harvest them before the flower stalk appears.

DESCRIPTION: Both species of salsify have grass-like leaves. Oyster plant (*T. porrifolius*) has hollow, unbranched stems. The daisy-like, pink or purple flowers grow to 4 inches (10 cm) wide and close by afternoon. They bloom from late spring to mid-summer. Green, spike-like bracts extend beyond the pink part of the flower. Yellow goatsbeard (*T. pratensis*) is similar, but the flowers are yellow and the stem is filled with a milky sap. It blooms from early summer through midfall.

HEIGHT: Oyster plant grows 2–5 feet (60–150 cm) tall; yellow goatsbeard reaches 1–3 feet (30–90 cm) tall.

PREFERRED SITE AND CLIMATE: Both species of salsify adapt to a wide range of soil conditions along roadsides and in unmowed areas throughout the United States.

LIFE CYCLE: Biennial.

HOW IT SPREADS: By seed.

SUGGESTED CONTROLS: Mulch to prevent existing seeds from sprouting. Hoe, pull, or flame seedlings as soon as you spot them. Pull, cut, or mow second-year plants before they set seed; repeat every week or two until plants stop resprouting. Or dig plants to make sure you get the taproot.

COMMENTS: The root of both species is edible. Harvest it before the plant sends up its second-year flower stalk, then peel it, cut it into chunks, and boil it.

Tribulus terrestris Zygophyllaceae

PUNCTURE VINE

Puncture vine gets its name from its sharp-spined seedpods. Each seedpod has five spiked burs that are hard enough to penetrate shoes and even tires!

OTHER COMMON NAMES: Burnut.

DESCRIPTION: Puncture vine has long, slender stems that trail on the ground to form a dense mat. Leaves consist of many pairs of small, oblong, hairy leaflets attached in pairs to the leaf stem. Small, yellow flowers with five petals bloom all summer in the leaf axils (where the leaves join the stem). The seedpods have five burs, each with two long, hard, sharp spines.

HEIGHT: The trailing stems can reach 6–8 feet (1.8–2.4 m) long.

PREFERRED SITE AND CLIMATE: Puncture vine usually grows in dry soil in unmowed areas and along roadsides in all but the most northern states.

LIFE CYCLE: Annual.

HOW IT SPREADS: By seed.

SUGGESTED CONTROLS: Mulch to prevent existing seeds from sprouting. Hoe, pull, or flame seedlings as soon as you spot them. Pull, cut, or mow larger plants; make sure you catch them before they set seed, or you'll have to deal with the spiny seedpods!

Trifolium repens   Leguminosae   *Tussilago farfara*   Compositae

WHITE CLOVER

COLTSFOOT

White clover adds nitrogen to the soil, making it a useful "pest." Consider living with it—in your lawn, at least— instead of trying to get rid of it.

The yellow flowers of coltsfoot bloom before the leaves emerge in spring. The flowers and seed heads look very much like those of dandelion.

OTHER COMMON NAMES: White Dutch clover.

DESCRIPTION: White clover is a common lawn plant with low stems that creep close to the ground. The leaves are made up of three rounded leaflets, each with a pale, V-shaped mark. White, ball-shaped flowers about ¾ inch (18 mm) in diameter bloom on a slender stem from spring through midfall.

HEIGHT: Some plants may grow to 1 foot (30 cm) tall in unmowed areas; in lawns, they usually adapt to whatever mowing height you use.

PREFERRED SITE AND CLIMATE: White clover comes up in lawns, gardens, and unmowed areas in the eastern half of the United States and in the Pacific Northwest.

LIFE CYCLE: Perennial.

HOW IT SPREADS: By seed and stolons (creeping aboveground stems). The seed is often carried in compost made from manure from animals that have fed on clover pastures or hay.

SUGGESTED CONTROLS: Keep the lawn at the tallest height in its accepted range to shade out the clover. Apply an organic fertilizer containing nitrogen, which inhibits white clover. In gardens and other areas, mulch to prevent existing seeds from sprouting. Hoe, pull, or flame seedlings as soon as you spot them. Pull or dig larger plants before they flower and set seed.

DESCRIPTION: Coltsfoot has thick, rubbery, round to heart-shaped leaves that are 4–8 inches (10–20 cm) wide or more. The leaves have woolly undersides and arise from the base of the plant on long leaf stems; they appear after the flowers. Early-blooming flowers to 2 inches (5 cm) wide resemble light yellow dandelions, with narrow ray flowers (petals). They bloom on scaly, leafless, woolly stems that have a purplish tinge.

HEIGHT: This weed grows 6–18 inches (15–45 cm) tall.

PREFERRED SITE AND CLIMATE: Coltsfoot can adapt to a wide range of soil conditions along roadsides and in unmowed areas in the northeastern United States.

LIFE CYCLE: Perennial.

HOW IT SPREADS: By seed and creeping roots.

SUGGESTED CONTROLS: Dig plants to get the creeping stems (let them dry out thoroughly in the sun before you compost them), or cut the stems to the ground. If you hoe, mow, or cut the plants, you'll need to do it again every 1–2 weeks until the roots stop resprouting. Or cover the roots with a dense mulch, such as newspaper, cardboard, or plastic, for one growing season.

| *Typha latifolia* | Typhaceae | *Urtica dioica* | Urticaceae |

COMMON CATTAIL

STINGING NETTLE

Common cattail spreads by rhizomes (creeping underground stems) and normally grows in patches. Controlling established clumps of this plant demands persistence.

Stinging nettle has stem and leaf hairs that contain formic acid, which causes a burning, stinging sensation when it touches your skin.

OTHER COMMON NAMES: Nail-rod, bulrush.

DESCRIPTION: This grass-like wetlands plant has a tall, stout stem. The flattened, gray-green leaves are about ¼–1 inch (6–25 mm) wide. The late-spring through midsummer flower is a brownish, sausage-shaped, squishy, fuzzy spike.

HEIGHT: Plants reach 40–100 inches (1–2.5 m) tall.

PREFERRED SITE AND CLIMATE: Common cattail is often seen growing in swamps, ditches, and shallow water throughout the United States.

LIFE CYCLE: Perennial.

HOW IT SPREADS: By seed or rhizomes.

SUGGESTED CONTROLS: This weed is usually tough to get rid of as long as the soil stays moist. If you do need to control it, cut the plants to the ground every week or two until the roots stop resprouting. Or cut the plants to the ground and cover the area with a dense mulch, such as cardboard, heavy plastic, landscape fabric, or old carpeting, for at least one growing season.

COMMENTS: The leaves can be used to weave baskets or chair seats.

OTHER SPECIES:
T. augustifolia, narrow-leaved cattail, is 2–5 feet (60 cm–1.5 m) tall. It prefers alkaline waters in the eastern United States, except in the Deep South.

DESCRIPTION: The stem and leaves of this antisocial weed are covered with hairs that cause inflammation or welts when touched. Dark green, rough, pointed leaves with toothed edges attach in pairs to the upright, slender, stiff stem. Petal-less, green flowers bloom in clusters in the leaf axils (where the leaves join the stem) from early summer through early fall. Plants often grow in patches.

HEIGHT: Stems grow 2–7 feet (60–200 cm) tall.

PREFERRED SITE AND CLIMATE: Stinging nettle pops up in rich, damp soil in woods, unmowed areas, and fencerows and along roadsides in the eastern three-quarters of the United States.

LIFE CYCLE: Perennial.

HOW IT SPREADS: By seed and rhizomes (creeping underground stems).

SUGGESTED CONTROLS: Always wear gloves when working around fresh nettles. Pull, hoe, mow, or cut seedlings as soon as you spot them. Dig plants to get the creeping stems (let them dry out thoroughly in the sun before you compost them), or cut the stems to the ground. If you hoe, mow, or cut the plants, you'll need to do it again every 1–2 weeks until the roots stop resprouting. Or cover the roots with a dense mulch, such as newspaper, cardboard, or plastic, for one growing season.

COMMENTS: The new shoots are edible when cooked (cooking deactivates the irritant).

MULLEINS

HOARY VERVAIN

Moth mullein produces thin, airy spikes of flat-faced flowers in summer to early fall. The flowers are usually yellow or white but may also be pink or pale orange.

Hoary vervain has upright stems topped with thin spikes of tiny, purplish flowers through summer. Dig out as many of the roots as you can, or smother them with a dense mulch.

DESCRIPTION: Mulleins have a rosette of leaves the first year and send up a spike of (usually) yellow flowers in early summer through early fall the second year. Moth mullein (*V. blattaria*) has a thin stem that may have hairs near the top. The lower leaves form a rosette that is about 8–24 inches (20–60 cm) wide. The dark green leaves may be slightly hairy and toothed or lobed; the upper leaves are pointed. Common mullein (*V. thapsus*) has a rosette of woolly leaves the first year. The second year it produces a tall, thick, woolly stem that usually doesn't branch. The leaves are light green and woolly. The lower ones are 6–18 inches (15–45 cm) long, while the upper ones are smaller. Yellow flowers with five lobes form on a thick, tall spike.

HEIGHT: Moth mullein grows 2–4 feet (60–120 cm) tall; common mullein grows 3–6 feet (90–180 cm) tall.

PREFERRED SITE AND CLIMATE: Mulleins are a common sight along dry, gravelly roadsides and in fencerows throughout the United States.

LIFE CYCLE: Biennial.

HOW IT SPREADS: By seed.

SUGGESTED CONTROLS: Mulch to prevent existing seeds from sprouting. Hoe, pull, or flame seedlings as soon as you spot them. Dig out the taproot, or pull, cut, or mow second-year plants before they set seed; repeat every week or two, if necessary, until the root stops resprouting.

DESCRIPTION: Hoary vervain has an upright, branched stem covered with white hairs. Leaves covered with white hairs and toothed edges attach directly to the stem, without a leaf stalk. The small, purplish flowers bloom in slender spikes from early summer through early fall.

HEIGHT: Hoary vervain grows 1–4 feet (30–120 cm) tall.

PREFERRED SITE AND CLIMATE: Hoary vervain is found along roadsides and in unmowed areas in the Midwest, the Great Plains, and Texas and along the Pacific coast.

LIFE CYCLE: Perennial.

HOW IT SPREADS: By seed and rhizomes (creeping underground stems).

SUGGESTED CONTROLS: Mulch to prevent existing seeds from sprouting. Hoe, pull, or flame seedlings as soon as you spot them. Dig larger plants to get the rhizomes (let them dry out thoroughly in the sun before you compost them), or cut the stems to the ground. If you hoe, mow, or cut the plants, you'll need to do it again every 1–2 weeks until the roots stop resprouting. Or cover the roots with a dense mulch, such as newspaper, cardboard, or plastic, for one growing season.

OTHER SPECIES:

V. bracteata, prostrate vervain, has hairy, creeping stems with rough, lobed leaves. Control this annual by pulling or cutting before it sets seed.

| *Veronica* spp. | Scrophulariaceae | *Viola* spp. | Violaceae |

SPEEDWELLS

VIOLETS

Veronicas are low-growing and have four-petaled, blue, purple, or white flowers. Some produce flowers in spikes; others bloom along the stem.

Sweet violet is charming but can also be a pest when it spreads out of control. Site it where the spread isn't a problem, or dig, cut, or smother unwanted plants.

DESCRIPTION: Common speedwell (*V. officinalis*) grows along the ground; the stem is thick and hairy. Elliptical leaves with toothed edges grow in pairs along the stem. Flowers bloom on upright stems in dense spikes from late spring through midsummer. Purslane speedwell (*V. peregrina*) has many upright stems that branch from the base. Narrow leaves have toothed edges at the base of the plant and attach in pairs to the stem; leaves at the top of the plant have smooth edges and alternate along the stem. Small white flowers bloom along the stem from early spring through late summer.

HEIGHT: Common speedwell is usually less than 1 inch (2.5 cm) tall; purslane speedwell grows to about 8 inches (20 cm) tall.

PREFERRED SITE AND CLIMATE: Common speedwell grows in stony or gravelly, acid soil in the northeastern and northcentral states. Purslane speedwell grows in damp soil in the eastern half of the United States, the most northern states in the western United States, and western Colorado.

LIFE CYCLE: Purslane speedwell is annual; common speedwell is perennial.

HOW IT SPREADS: By seed.

SUGGESTED CONTROLS: Mulch to prevent existing seeds from sprouting. Pull, cut, or mow plants every week or two until they stop resprouting, or cover the area with a dense mulch.

DESCRIPTION: Sweet, or garden, violet (*V. odorata*) has heart- or kidney-shaped leaves. The fragrant spring flowers are ¾ inch (18 mm) wide; they are usually deep purple but can be white or pink. The flower has a short, nearly straight spur. Some types may have double flowers. Common blue, or woolly, violet (*V. papilionacea*) has heart-shaped leaves. The leaf stalks are longer than the flower stalks and may be downy. The flowers bloom from spring through early summer.

HEIGHT: Violets grow 6–12 inches (15–30 cm) tall.

PREFERRED SITE AND CLIMATE: These charming but invasive plants thrive in rich, moist soil in semishade. They pop up in lawns, flower beds, and open woodlands in the eastern United States and along the Pacific coast.

LIFE CYCLE: Perennial.

HOW IT SPREADS: Sweet violet spreads by stolons (creeping aboveground stems) and common blue violet spreads by rhizomes (creeping underground stems).

SUGGESTED CONTROLS: Dig out the plants, getting as much of the root system as you can. (Let the roots dry thoroughly in the sun before composting them.) Cut down or hoe new shoots that appear every week or two until they stop resprouting. Or cut them to the ground, then cover with a dense mulch, such as cardboard, newspaper, or plastic, for one growing season.

WILD GRAPES

Several similar species of wild grapes can be weed problems. Coiled tendrils at the leaf axils (where the leaves join the stem) help these vines climb plants and fences.

DESCRIPTION: The rough, heart-shaped or triangular leaves of wild grapes are 1–4 inches (2.5–10 cm) wide, with toothed edges. They alternate on the slender, woody, vining stem. Inconspicuous clusters of five-petaled flowers form a loose spike in summer, followed by soft, round, purple berries.

HEIGHT: Vines can grow to 60 feet (18 m) tall or more.

PREFERRED SITE AND CLIMATE: Wild grapes grow along shady roadsides and borders of woods throughout the United States.

LIFE CYCLE: Perennial.

HOW IT SPREADS: By seed.

SUGGESTED CONTROLS: Hoe, pull, or flame seedlings as soon as you spot them. Cut the stems back to the ground every week or two until they stop resprouting; persistence is the key to control. Or cut them to the ground, then cover the area with a dense mulch, such as cardboard, plastic, or landscape fabric, for at least one growing season.

COMMENTS: If you have lots of grapevines, consider using them for crafts. They make wonderful wreaths and can also be used for weaving baskets.

COMMON COCKLEBUR

Common cocklebur is an annual weed that grows throughout most of the United States. Its seeds are spread by hooked burs that cling to fur and fabric.

DESCRIPTION: Common cocklebur has triangular, slightly lobed leaves with long leaf stems. The leaves alternate along a rough or hairy, ridged main stem that sometimes has spots. Plants bloom from late summer through midfall. The seeds are borne in an oval, prickly bur that turns woody and brown as the seed matures.

HEIGHT: Stems can reach 2–4 feet (60–120 cm) tall.

PREFERRED SITE AND CLIMATE: Common cocklebur grows on low ground, along roadsides, and in unmowed areas with poor soil throughout the United States, except in northern New England.

LIFE CYCLE: Annual.

HOW IT SPREADS: By seed.

SUGGESTED CONTROLS: Mulch to prevent existing seeds from sprouting. Hoe, pull, or flame seedlings as soon as you spot them. Pull, cut, or mow larger plants before the burs form.

COMMENTS: Common cocklebur can be confused with common burdock (*Arctium minus*), described on page 92, but the burs of cocklebur are long, while those of burdock are round.

ACKNOWLEDGMENTS

Photo Credits

Addington Turf & Horticultural Consultants: photographer Kenneth R. Smith: pages 87 (right) and 91 (left).

William H. Allen, Jr.: page 90 (left).

Ardea, London: photographer Elizabeth S. Burgess: page 113 (right).

Auscape: photographer John McCammon: front cover.

A–Z Botanical: pages 86 (left), 106 (right), and 111 (right); photographer Ron Bass: pages 135 (left) and 143 (right); photographers F. Collet & U. Lund: page 110 (right); photographer Anthony Cooper: page 24 (bottom); photographer Jennifer Fry: page 155 (left); photographer Derek Gould: page 111 (left); photographer Geoff Kidd: page 116 (left); photographer G. A. Matthews: page 140 (left); photographer Maurice Nimmo: page 145 (right); photographer Annie Poole: page 89 (left); photographer Malcolm Richards: page 97 (left); photographer Anthony Seinet: page 94 (right).

Gillian Beckett: pages 85 (right), 102 (right), 105 (left), 113 (left), 115 (left), 117 (left), 119 (right), 124 (right), 127 (left), 144 (left), 145 (left), 146 (right), 147 (right), 148 (left), and 151 (left).

Bruce Coleman Ltd: photographer John R. Anthony: page 12; photographers Bob & Clara Calhoun: opposite contents page; photographer Patrick Clement: page 75 (bottom right); photographer Eric Crichton: page 75 (top left); photographer Sir Jeremy Grayson: contents page (top) and page 58 (top right); photographer Werner Layer: page 94 (left); photographer Dr. Eckart Pott: page 21 (bottom); photographer Hans Reinhard: pages 16 (top), 29 (bottom), 41 (bottom), 49 (right), 69 (top right and bottom), and 143 (left); photographer John Shaw: opposite title page; photographer Michel Viard: endpapers.

Thomas Eltzroth: back cover (top), pages 11 (left and right), 46 (bottom), 87 (left), 88 (left), 104 (left), 109 (left), 125 (left and right), 132 (right), 134 (right), 138 (right), 149 (left), and 152 (left).

Derek Fell: back cover (bottom), pages 112 (right) and 136 (left).

The Garden Picture Library: photographer Clive Boursnell: page 27; photographer Lynne Brotchie: page 26 (top); photographer Brian Carter: pages 15 (bottom right), 79 (left), and 82; photographer Geoff Dann: page 139 (left); photographer David England: page 81 (top right); photographer Christopher Fairweather: page 51 (left); photographer John Glover: page 35 (bottom); photographer Marijke Heuff: pages 15 (bottom left) and 72; photographer Neil Holmes: page 29 (top); photographer Michael Howes: pages 26 (bottom), 28 (bottom), 42, and 57 (top left); photographer Lamontagne: pages 8, 15 (top left), and 39 (right); photographer Jane Legate: page 78 (bottom left); photographers Mayer /Le Scanff: pages 18 (bottom), 34, and 64; photographer Jerry Pavia: pages 46 (top) and 50 (right); photographer Gary Rogers: page 130 (left); photographer J. S. Sira: title page; photographer Brigitte Thomas: page 39 (left); photographer Mel Watson: page 66 (bottom left); photographer Steven Wooster: page 47 (right).

Holt Studios International: photographer Nigel Cattlin: contents page (center), pages 76 (bottom right), 78 (top), 84 (left), 86 (right), 89 (right), 90 (right), 92 (right), 93 (left), 95 (left), 96 (right), 99 (left), 100 (left), 101 (left and right), 103 (left and right), 104 (right), 106 (left), 107 (left and right), 108 (right), 110 (left), 115 (right), 120 (right), 122 (left and right), 123 (left), 126 (right), 128 (right), 129 (right), 130 (right), 132 (left), 133 (left), 134 (left), 136 (right), 139 (right), 141 (right), 142 (right), 146 (left), 147 (left), 151 (right), and 152 (right); photographer John Henry Galindo: page 102 (left); photographer Bob Gibbons: page 41 (top); photographer Rosemary Mayer: page 95 (right); photographer Gordon Roberts: pages 48 (center) and 124 (left); photographer Duncan Smith: page 123 (right).

S & O Mathews: pages 15 (top right), 20 (right), 24 (top), 38 (top), 40 (top), 45 (left and right), 56 (top), 57 (top right), 58 (bottom), 60 (top), 61 (top right), 70, 76 (top), 77 (top), 99 (right), 131 (left), and 154 (left).

Clive Nichols: copyright page, pages 18 (top), 19, 22, 40 (bottom), 49 (left), 52, 55 (left and right), 57 (bottom), 58 (top left), 61 (bottom right), 63, 71 (top), 79 (right), and 84 (right).

Nancy J. Ondra: page 149 (right).

Jerry Pavia: pages 56 (bottom), 61 (top left), and 76 (bottom left).

Penn. State Weed Science: photographer Nathan Hartwig: pages 114 (right), 116 (right), 128 (left), 129 (left), and 133 (right).

Photos Horticultural: back cover (center), half title page, pages 14 (top), 16 (bottom), 20 (left), 21 (top), 25, 28 (top), 33, 35 (top), 36 (left and right), 37 (top and bottom), 38 (bottom left, bottom center, and bottom right), 48 (top, bottom left, and bottom right), 50 (left), 51 (right), 54 (left, center, and right), 59, 60 (bottom), 61 (bottom left), 62 (top and bottom), 66 (top and bottom right), 67, 69 (top left), 71 (bottom), 74, 77 (bottom left and bottom right), 78 (bottom right), 80, 81 (top left), 85 (left), 97 (right), 118 (right), 138 (left), 140 (right), and 144 (right).

Lorna Rose: pages 75 (top right) and 81 (bottom).

Harry Smith Collection: pages 88 (right), 91 (right), 92 (left), 93 (right), 96 (left), 98 (left and right), 100 (right), 105 (right), 108 (left), 112 (left), 114 (left), 118 (left), 119 (left), 120 (left), 121 (left and right), 126 (left), 131 (right), 135 (right), 137 (left and right), 141 (left), 142 (left), 148 (right), 150 (left and right), 153 (left and right), 154 (right), and 155 (right).

Weldon Russell: contents page (bottom), pages 17, 47 (left), 75 (bottom left), and 117 (right).

Zeneca Ltd: pages 109 (right) and 127 (right).